Britain 1815–51: Protest and Reform

Martin Collier and
Philip Pedley

Series Editors
Martin Collier
Erica Lewis
Rosemary Rees

Heinemann

Heinemann Educational Publishers
Halley Court, Jordan Hill, Oxford, OX2 8EJ
a division of Reed Educational & Professional Publishing Ltd
Heinemann is a registered trademark of Reed Educational & Professional
Publishing Ltd

OXFORD MELBOURNE AUCKLAND
JOHANNESBURG BLANTYRE GABORONE
IBADAN PORTSMOUTH NH (USA) CHICAGO

© Heinemann Educational Publishers 2001

First published 2001

ISBN 0 435 32716 X
03 02 01
10 9 8 7 6 5 4 3 2

Typeset and illustrated by Wyvern 21 Ltd, Bristol

Printed and bound in Great Britain by The Bath Press Ltd, Bath

Picture research by Thelma Gilbert

Photographic acknowledgements
The authors and publisher would like to thank the following for
permission to reproduce photographs: British Library: 83; Hulton Getty:
5, 39, 68, 74, 87 (bottom), 95, 110, 119, 127; Mary Evans Picture
Library: 32, 87 (top), 89, 101, 134, 135, 194; Punch: 85, 138

Cover photograph: © Mary Evans Picture Library

Dedicated to Olivia

CONTENTS

A2 SECTION: ANALYSIS AND INTERPRETATION

Britain in the age of reform, 1815–51

HOW TO USE THIS BOOK

The book is divided into an AS section and an A2 section and each has been written in a distinct style. The AS section is written as a descriptive analysis. Many of the key aspects of British social, political and economic development are tackled in this section. The questions at the end of each chapter aim to challenge the students to use the information in the chapter to analyse, prioritise and explain the important aspects of the subject. It is hoped that by reading each chapter, discussing key issues and answering the summary questions students will acquire a clear understanding of each topic.

The A2 section of the book is more analytical in style. It deals with the themes and issues of the period that are included in the Awarding Bodies' specifications. Students who use the book as part of their A2 studies should also read through the relevant chapters in the AS section of the book. An example of this is that students who are studying the Chartists at A2 level should not only read Section 5, but also Chapter 10 of the book. The A2 section has been written in such a way that it will also be useful for those AS students who wish to extend their understanding of the subject.

At the end of each of the AS and A2 sections there are Assessment Sections. These are based on the requirements of the new AS and A2 specifications provided by the three Awarding Bodies: Edexcel, AQA and OCR. There are exam-style source and essay questions for each specification. There then follows detailed guidance on how students might answer the questions together with sample answers.

AS SECTION: ECONOMIC, SOCIAL AND POLITICAL CHANGE IN BRITAIN, 1815–51

INTRODUCTION

In the period 1815–51 Britain experienced considerable economic, social and political change. Industrialisation, the legacy of the Napoleonic wars and the development of new political ideas were all to have a considerable impact on this period of British history.

Economic change. Despite an economic depression that followed the Napoleonic wars, Britain experienced a period of rapid economic change. The move from **cottage industry** to factory continued with the widespread implementation of new machinery, such as the **power loom**. The introduction, construction and operation of the railways were to have a considerable impact on the British economy and society as a whole.

Social change. Rapid population growth and urbanisation were to create widespread social problems. Poor public health, housing and poverty were to lead to some change in attitudes about the responsibility of the government in dealing with social problems. However, the period was dominated by the idea of *laissez-faire*: that the state should not intervene in the economy. Some campaigners such as Lord Shaftesbury or Edwin Chadwick pressed for government intervention to improve the condition of factory and mine workers and also the poor. The period in question saw changes in attitude towards the Established Church (the Church of England) and attempts to reform its worst excesses. There were also limited attempts at providing basic education for the poor. However, such attempts were very restricted by the opposition of both the established and nonconformist churches and a widespread belief in *laissez-faire*.

Political change. The changes described above created an atmosphere in which demands for the reform of the political system increased. Radical agitation in the post-Napoleonic war period came to a head in the Peterloo demonstration in 1819 at which a number of demonstrators were massacred. The calls for reform were met with a combination of repression and reform. From 1822 a period of what is known as 'Liberal Toryism' resulted in a series of financial, trade and legal reforms. In 1832 a Whig government introduced a limited reform of the franchise through the introduction of the Great Reform Act. Further reforms by the Whigs included the introduction of a new Poor Law in 1834.

The late 1830s saw economic depression and the growth of radical protest groups which demanded further reform. Significant among these groups were the Chartists, the Anti-Corn Law League and the Ten-Hour Movement. Such agitation was deflected by the actions of government and the improvement in economic conditions. From 1841 a government led by Sir Robert Peel introduced free trade measures culminating in the repeal of the Corn Laws in 1846.

Foreign policy. Throughout the period in question, successive British governments followed a foreign policy that attempted to maintain the settlement agreed with other powers at the Congress of Vienna in 1815. They also attempted to uphold the basic principles of foreign policy:

* maintaining the balance of power
* protection of trade
* isolation from foreign entanglements.

CHAPTER 1

What were the reasons for and extent of economic change, 1800–51?

POPULATION

Historians are agreed that a key element in explaining the extent of economic change in the period from 1815 to 1851 was the rapid growth in population. The increase in the population during this period was both significant and remarkable.

The population of Britain and rates of population growth, 1820–51

	Population of UK (in millions)	Percentage rate of growth of population
1821	14.21	17
1831	16.37	15.2
1841	18.55	13.3
1851	20.88	12.6

(Source: B.R. Mitchell and P. Deane, *Abstract of British Historical Statistics*, Cambridge, 1962, pp. 8–10.)

Why did the population increase?

The causes of this rise in the population have been the subject of historical controversy. From 1801 the national **census** has given the historian a fairly accurate series of statistics. However, from 1801 to 1831 the census was undertaken by local officials – usually Poor Law overseers – and it is quite likely that the figures are incomplete. In 1836 the Civil Registration Act made compulsory the registration of births, deaths and marriages so the 1841 census was the first which could be checked. Therefore, the reliability of the statistical data is a problem for the historian until close to the middle of the century.

The argument that the population rose because the **death rate** fell following medical and other social improvements is difficult to prove. More likely, the population rose because of the increase in fertility due to an increase in the numbers marrying at an earlier age. These factors meant that women had more children during their lifetime. This is called an increase in **fecundity**. The explanation for these trends was an increase in economic opportunity arising from the changes explained below. From around 1700 to 1851 the numbers of those not marrying fell from 15 per cent to 7 per cent and during the same period the average first age of marriage came down from 26.5 to 23.5 years. Better wages in industry, the growth of the towns and cities and the decline in apprenticeships are all of real importance in explaining why the population rose.

Urbanisation

The new towns and cities attracted the young with the prospect of stable jobs and higher wages. This had a significant effect on the marriage rates. The result was an explosion in the population of the newly urbanised areas despite the poor living conditions to be found in many of them. In **Manchester** the population nearly doubled from 135,000 in 1821 to 235,000 in 1841; a figure matched by Glasgow which saw an increase from 147,000 in 1821 to 287,000 in 1841. Some of this growth was a result of migration. Seasonal work and good job prospects attracted significant numbers of Irish immigrants to industrial centres; in 1825 there were 35,000 Irish migrants living in Manchester. The numbers crossing the Irish Sea increased with improvements in transport: for example, in 1818 the ferry service between Glasgow and Belfast was opened. By the 1830s fares were as low as 3d for the crossing. Irish migrants were also encouraged by domestic problems such as the failed rebellion of 1798. The famine in the 1840s led to an influx of around 1.4 million between 1846 and 1851. As transport improved, most importantly with the development of cheap railway services from the 1830s, so the possibility of movement increased. However, migration was only a secondary factor to the increase in fecundity in explaining population growth.

Changes in the textile industry

By 1820 the process of spinning most textiles such as cotton, silk or wool had become factory based. The invention of the **mule** by Samuel Crompton had made this possible as had the work of Richard Roberts between 1825 and 1830 in making the mule fully automatic. Change also took place in the weaving of textiles. By 1820 there were 14,000 **power looms** in operation as opposed to some 240,000 hand looms. The imbalance was caused by the problems in adapting power looms to different styles and qualities of cloth. Also, the low wages of the **hand loom weavers** made change less necessary, wage rates falling from a peak of 23 shillings per week in 1805 to 6 shillings per week in 1831. Therefore, most mill owners employed both power and hand looms. However, in times of economic depression, it was the hand loom which was deprived of work first: in 1825 over 250,000 weavers were made redundant as the result of a slump in the market for their cloth.

The move towards larger cotton factories was partly the result of a shift from water to steam power. Before improvements in steam engine technology, most of the new factories such as Richard Arkwright's 1771 factory at Cromford (Derbyshire) relied on water power.

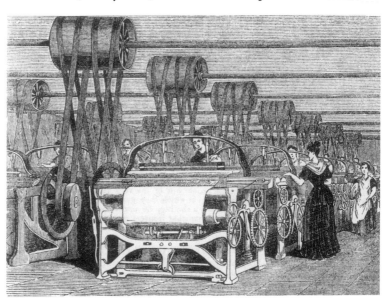

Power looms driven by belts running from overhead transmission shafts.

Horsepower used in textile factories

| | Cotton | | Woollen and Worsted | |
	Steam	Water	Steam	Water
1838	46,826	17,389	17,389	10,405
1850	71,005	11,500	23,345	10,314

(Source: A.E. Musson, *The Growth of British Industry*, Batsford, 1978, p. 112.)

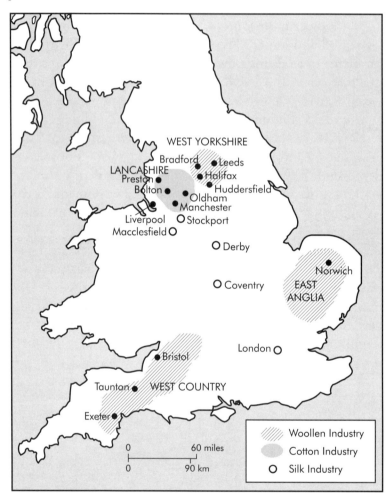

The location of the wool and cotton industries in the 1830s.

Factory location. The result of this shift from water to steam power was the relocation of factories from country areas into towns and cities. Of 1600 cotton mills in England in 1838 some 1200 were based in Lancashire. Many of the larger factories undertook the spinning and weaving process at one location. This was an important innovation and led to the creation of some large-scale enterprises: a company such as Horrocks employed over

300 workers at its factory in Preston. The shift away from hand loom weaving continued. As the power loom became more technically reliable, so the hand loom was used more for producing cloth which was technically difficult to make or needed to be of a higher quality than the power looms could produce. By 1851 the balance of power looms to hand looms in the cotton industry was 250,000 to 43,000. Overall, the growth of the cotton industry in the period was spectacular. In 1811 the industry imported 62 million **lb** of raw cotton to process into cotton cloth; by 1841 that figure had risen to 520 million lb. Because the innovations in machinery were more suitable to the cotton industry than any other, so it was cotton that became the first industry to move to a factory system on a large scale.

Wool and other textiles. The growth in other textile industries was not so spectacular. The woollen industry was established in England hundreds of years before cotton but wool was less suited to power-driven machinery. Early wool factories such as Benjamin Gott's Park Mills in Leeds concentrated on the preparatory processes such as **scribbling** and **carding** rather than mechanised spinning or weaving. By 1851 there were still only 9500 power looms weaving wool; early power looms strained the wool thereby causing the wool fibres to snap. This accounts for the fact that in the mid-1840s there were still 800,000 workers engaged in hand loom weaving and many of them in the woollen industry.

Worsted, silk and linen. The **worsted** industry adapted more easily to the new technology because of the strength of the fibre. It relocated around Bradford where there was a good supply of coal to fuel steam-driven machinery. While in the worsted, silk and linen industries there were factory units, most textile manufacture continued to be workshop based. In the silk industry, weaving machines were not introduced until the 1850s. In the manufacture of linen, spinning technology was mechanised, there being 965,000 spindles, many in the north of Ireland around Belfast. However, the number of power looms in the linen industry was limited to 1200 in 1850. As with so many other textile industries, the improvements in technology were insufficient to make the industry completely factory based.

KEY TERMS

lb signifies a pound in weight in the Imperial system. One lb is equal to 0.45 kg.

Scribbling The process whereby the wool is prepared for the manufacturing process.

Carding The process by which wool fibres are straightened out and are made ready for spinning. It was originally done by hand. Eventually the process was mechanised by Richard Arkwright's carding machine.

Worsted A fine woollen cloth which was originally made in Norfolk.

The growth of the coal industry

Increasing demand for coal. The production of coal rose as demand grew because of the following factors:

- a growing population,
- the use of steam power
- gas lighting
- a larger export market.

In response to the increase in demand, deeper mines were dug. The railways in the 1830s and 1840s provided a great stimulus to the industry and opened up production in more remote areas since, if linked to a railway, transport costs were cheap. Most coal was still produced for the home market until 1834 when the government repealed the general export duty. As a result, demand for coal for export increased. In 1820 around 0.3 million tons or 1.7 per cent of coal produced was exported; by 1850 this figure had risen to 3.2 million tons (6.5 per cent). The introduction of coal gas lighting also increased demand for coal during this period: by 1859 there were around 1000 gasworks nationwide.

Innovation in the coal industry. To increase the production of coal, certain problems associated with digging deeper mines had to be resolved.

- *Explosions.* The problem of **explosions underground** was tackled by **John Buddle** who in 1810 attempted to use trap doors to introduce fresh air to various points in the mine. Buddle also introduced the concept of a mechanical ventilator to pump stale and potentially explosive air out of the pit. However, his innovation needed considerable refinement and it was not until 1849 that William Brunton successfully used a fan to ventilate the mines.
- *Light.* To improve the safety when using light in the mines, Sir Humphrey Davy introduced a new lamp in 1815. The Davy Lamp worked on the simple principle of using a gauze to surround the light, thereby preventing heat from escaping and causing an explosion. However, as with Buddle's innovation, it took a considerable amount of time before such a change was universally used or accepted.

Total UK coal output, 1820–50

Year	Coal output (million tons)
1820	17.4
1830	23
1846	44
1850	49.4

(Adapted from P. Mathias, *The First Industrial Nation*, Routledge, 1969, p. 449. Quoted from Mitchell and Deane.)

KEY THEME

Explosions underground
These were caused by the building up of stale and potentially explosive gases underground.

KEY PERSON

John Buddle was the leading colliery engineer of the time.

As the Royal Commission report of 1840 showed, the mines were **labour intensive** and made extensive use of female and child labour. They were also dangerous. Significantly, however, the basic technology used to mine coal did not change throughout the period.

The iron industry

In the iron industry, any technological changes were minor in comparison to the **innovations of the eighteenth century**. The main changes were in the *scale* of production, as in coal. In the smelting process, the size of blast furnaces increased considerably. At the beginning of the nineteenth century, furnaces in the Black Country were producing an average 30 tons a week. Two decades later, that figure had risen to 50 tons a week and higher. The introduction of the hot blast process in smelting, patented by James Neilson in 1828, helped to reduce the cost of the process by over one-third. As a result, the Scottish iron industry, which had previously suffered from the handicap of coal which was low in carbon, received a significant boost. Production increased from 25,000 tons of pig iron in 1825 to 500,000 tons by 1848.

Agriculture

Despite the rapid growth of industry, until 1851 most people continued to live and work on the land. The condition of agriculture, therefore, was vital to the economic well-being of the people.

Agricultural depression. Despite the protection given to agriculture by the **Corn Laws**, the price of wheat fell after 1815 from an average of 102.45 shillings a quarter in 1810–14 to 57.15 shillings a quarter in 1820–4. In 1822 the price of wheat fell as low as 43 shillings. This fall in prices was the result of too much wheat being produced. The distress at such a fall in income was felt in many areas. In 1816 there were riots in East Anglia. However, this was partly as a result of the 400,000 ex servicemen returning from the Napoleonic wars and joining what was a shrinking labour market. In *Rural Rides* (1830) William Cobbett described a bleak picture of agricultural depression with falling prices and high rents. In 1830 the **Captain Swing** riots took place across the wheat-growing south and

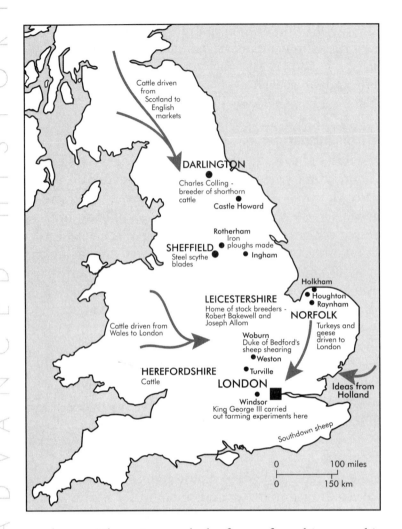

Cattle driven from Scotland to English markets

DARLINGTON

Charles Colling - breeder of shorthorn cattle

Castle Howard

Rotherham Iron ploughs made

SHEFFIELD
Steel scythe blades

Ingham

Holkham

Houghton
Raynham

LEICESTERSHIRE
Home of stock breeders - Robert Bakewell and Joseph Allom

NORFOLK

Cattle driven from Wales to London

Woburn
Duke of Bedford's sheep shearing

Turkeys and geese driven to London

Weston

HEREFORDSHIRE
Cattle

Turville

LONDON

Ideas from Holland

Windsor
King George III carried out farming experiments here

Southdown sheep

0   100 miles
|——————|
0   150 km

British agriculture, 1815–51, showing areas of farming innovation.

south-east. These riots took the form of machine wrecking and the burning of farms. They were caused by an accumulation of factors which included the prolonged depression and the resulting rural unemployment. However, the Swing riots were also aimed at rural injustice and the Game Laws of 1815 (which introduced harsh punishment for poaching) in particular.

High farming and improvements in agriculture. Not all agriculture suffered depression after 1815. Those farmers who invested in improvements and better farming techniques such as the use of machinery were able to counter falling prices with higher output.

- *Growth in demand.* There was growing demand for food with the population in England rising from 11 million

KEY TERMS

High farming The term was first used by James Caird in *English Agriculture in 1851–2*. In his book, Caird described high farmers as those who invested in new techniques of farming such as better drainage and farm management with the aim of increasing productivity.

Guano Bird droppings used as a natural fertiliser because of a high phosphate content.

in 1815 to 15 million in 1836. This demand was met by a 16 per cent increase in the amount of wheat grown per acre between 1815/19 and 1832/36.

- *Innovations.* Landowners introduced many of the changes associated with what became known as **high farming**, for example, the use of the fertiliser **guano** and the growing of a variety of crops.
- *The importance of soil.* Increased production was achieved by farmers who worked light soil. Soil was the key to success: innovation was far easier on the light soils of areas such as Norfolk. Crop rotations (putting different crops in different fields each year) and the mix of arable and pasture farming protected the farmers from relying solely on wheat prices.
- *The problems of heavy soils.* The heavy soils of counties such as Cambridgeshire and Huntingdonshire were unsuitable for fodder crops such as turnips. Crops were grown in the old three-crop rotation and wheat was the main cash crop. These soils were also unsuitable for sheep.
- *Price rises from the mid-1830s.* From the mid-1830s agricultural fortunes improved. The price of wheat began to rise as the growth in population soaked up the increases in supply; after 1837 the price often topped 60 shillings a quarter. This stimulated investment in improvement. However, that investment was often limited to larger farms.
- *Drainage.* In the heavy soil areas, output increased as a result of improvements in drainage. These included the introduction of steam pumps in the fens and cheap tile drains which improved underground drainage. In 1846 the Prime Minister Robert Peel introduced the Agricultural Drainage Act which provided government loans to landlords who drained their land.

SUMMARY QUESTIONS

1 Why did the population increase in the first half of the nineteenth century?

2 What was the nature and extent of economic change in the period, 1815–51?

3 Why were there so many problems in agriculture in the period, 1815–51?

CHAPTER 2

What were the reasons for, and what was the extent of, unrest, reform and reaction, 1815–20?

THE POLITICAL SYSTEM

Most MPs belonged to one of two aristocratic parties – **Whigs** and **Tories**. Originally terms of abuse, these labels came to denote the two rival parties of the eighteenth century.

As the constitutional debate had become less relevant by the end of the eighteenth century, party rivalry tended to give way to personal or factional politics. This was when groups formed governments based on loyalty to individuals rather than ideology. The hostility to the French Revolution and the wartime consensus further reduced ideological conflict.

After 1815 party rivalry increased, especially over the question of **parliamentary reform** which the Whigs favoured but which Tories steadfastly opposed. Some Tories did take a more sympathetic approach to both church and constitutional reform, but the **Ultras** remained implacably hostile.

THE CORN LAWS

The state of England in 1815

The end of the Napoleonic wars did not lead to the anticipated period of prosperity. Instead, the first years of peace were troubled by widespread popular discontent. This was partly due to the deep economic depression, the reasons for which were as follows:

• Government orders for military supplies fell.

- The employment situation was worsened by the return to Britain of some 400,000 demobilised soldiers looking for work.
- The long-term rise in population, the mechanisation in farming and traditional crafts, and the post-war recession led to rising unemployment and underemployment.
- Demand for British goods from the European continent remained weak.
- Prices of many goods also fell.

In the longer term, there were to be some positive consequences of the war. The way in which money had been raised to fight the war led to the creation of a large capital market in London. This meant that it was easier to borrow large amounts of money to invest in industry. The benefits of this were to be seen in the 1830s when the introduction of the railways created a vast demand for capital. However, the end of the war brought the prospect of change which worried many influential groups in society, including those involved in farming who feared a fall in prices.

The passage of the Corn Laws

Parliament in 1815 was dominated by landowners. During the Napoleonic wars wheat prices had been high. During the period 1810–14 wheat prices were an average 102.45 shillings a quarter, whereas in the period before the wars during 1790–4 average wheat prices were 49.57 shillings a quarter. The fear of many farmers, especially those landowning gentry who farmed wheat in the south of England, was that the end of the Napoleonic wars would result in Britain being flooded with cheap foreign wheat. This would reduce the price of wheat, which had been high during the wars. The problem for many farmers was that they borrowed heavily during the wars in order to increase production. The fear was that a reduction in price would leave them further in debt. Therefore, they persuaded Parliament to pass the **Corn Laws**. However, economic depression coincided with poor harvests in 1816 which led to the doubling of bread prices. Agitators hoping for political reform now the wars were over were able to blame short-term food shortages on the Corn Laws and the corrupt Parliament that passed them.

KEY FACTS

Demand for British goods
During the wars, Napoleon's blockade of Britain had meant that British manufacturers were unable to sell their goods on the continent. However, after the wars the European economy took some time to readjust and therefore British manufacturers still could not sell their goods to the continent.

The Corn Laws These laws prevented foreign wheat coming into Britain until the price of British wheat reached 80 shillings a quarter.

KEY DATES

The monarchy

George III	1760–1820
George IV	1820–30
William IV	1830–37
Victoria	1837–1901

RADICAL AGITATION

Unrest. There was widespread but unco-ordinated political agitation after 1815. Much of this protest was directed at immediate threats to individual well-being. Protesters demanded 'bread or blood' in East Anglia in 1816 and unemployed textile workers destroyed machinery in the Midlands. However, in this climate of social and economic distress **radicals** were also able to blame misgovernment by King George III and his aristocratic Tory government led by **Lord Liverpool**. The theme of the radicals was that the poor economic conditions were a result of corruption and political mismanagement. **Radical journalism** was significant at this time. In his weekly *Political Register* **William Cobbett** denounced the injustices and incompetence of aristocratic government. The radical leader **Henry 'Orator' Hunt** attacked the injustice of an unreformed political system at a large meeting in Spa Fields, London in 1816. Hunt stirred the crowd by linking their economic situation to political circumstances:

> What was the cause of the want of employment? Taxation. What was the cause of taxation? Corruption . . . [Taxes] were imposed by the authority of a group who thought of nothing but oppressing the people and living on the plunder gained from the people's miseries.

The plight of the hand loom weavers. One of the most serious centres of distress was Lancashire. The introduction of machines into textile factories, and especially the power loom, had a damaging impact on the fortunes of the cotton hand loom weavers. Slowly but surely they found themselves undercut by the new technology. Although they still found work in times of plenty, they were increasingly underemployed. In 1817 a group of weavers, the 'Blanketeers', optimistically aimed to march from Lancashire to petition Parliament about their misfortune. Although peaceful, the 'Blanketeers' were seen as a threat by the authorities and they were stopped at Stockport by a combination of local magistrates and cavalry from the militia.

Peterloo was so named by amalgamating the names St Peter's Field and Waterloo, scene of the recent victory over the French.

Legislatory attorney A lawyer who would represent the views of those without a vote.

Radical journalism
Cobbett's *Political Register* was an example of the radical newspapers and magazines published after the Napoleonic wars. The publications were widely read by the literate working class. Other examples were the *Manchester Observer*, first published in 1818, and William Sherwin's *Weekly Political Register*, first published in 1817.

Corrupt political system
The criticism of many who attacked the political system as it stood was that it only represented a few and that these few used it to improve their own lives but not the lives of others.

The Cato Street Conspiracy, 1820 The conspirators' plan included occupation of the Bank of England and the establishment of a provisional government. Thistlewood and four co-conspirators were executed at Newgate Gaol.

Peterloo. One of the most significant events during this period of unrest and disorder occurred on St Peter's Field, Manchester in 1819. The demands of the weavers for a minimum wage and an improvement in employment prospects were ignored by employers. This discontent with economic conditions turned many towards radical politics. A number of large demonstrations were held across Britain in the summer of 1819 to protest against the **corrupt political system**. In Birmingham in July 1819, Sir Charles Worsely was elected as '**legislatory attorney**' to represent those without the vote. At St Peter's Field, the local magistrates took fright at the size of the crowd. An attempt by the local yeomanry to arrest 'Orator' Hunt failed and the cavalry were called in to disperse the crowds. Their intervention led to the deaths of eleven people. The event was quickly dubbed the 'massacre of Peterloo'. The reaction of Hunt and other moderate reformers was to insist on 'passive resistance' and a demand for an enquiry into Peterloo. Other radicals such as Arthur Thistlewood hoped for more direct action. Thistlewood and his co-conspirators represented a violent wing of the radical movement. In February 1820 Thistlewood plotted an ambitious conspiracy to assassinate the whole cabinet in what became known as the **Cato Street Conspiracy**.

KEY DATES: The governments

Prime Minister	Party	Dates
Lord Liverpool	Tory	1812–April 1827
George Canning	Tory	April–Aug 1827
Viscount Goderich	Tory	Aug 1827–Jan 1828
Duke of Wellington	Tory	Jan 1828–Nov 1830
Earl Grey	Whig	Nov 1830–July 1834
Viscount Melbourne	Whig	July–Nov 1834
Duke of Wellington	Tory	Nov–Dec 1834
Sir Robert Peel	Conservative	Dec 1834–April 1835
Viscount Melbourne	Whig	April 1835–Aug 1841
Sir Robert Peel	Conservative	Aug 1841–June 1846
Lord John Russell	Whig	June 1846–Feb 1852

THE ATTITUDE OF LORD LIVERPOOL'S GOVERNMENT

The Tory government was reluctant to embark on any reform as long as social unrest and political agitation persisted. It is important to remember that the outlook of Lord Liverpool and ministers such as the Earl of Eldon and Viscount Sidmouth had been shaped by their hostility to the **French Revolution** and, lacking both imagination and accurate information, ministers were fearful of political upheaval. The priorities of the Tory government were the maintenance of law and order and the vigorous suppression of organised popular unrest. The suspension of **Habeas Corpus** in 1816, thus permitting arrest without trial, and the use of troops, spies and informers have given the early peacetime years of Tory rule a reputation for being **repressive**. The Six Acts passed in December 1819 in the wake of Peterloo have added to that reputation.

The Six Acts provided for the following:

- A speedy trial could be arranged for those accused in 'cases of misdemeanor'.
- Penalties for seditious libel were increased.
- The stamp duty was imposed on all periodicals. This was a blow to radical journalists.
- Public meetings were limited.
- The training of people in the use of firearms was forbidden.
- Magistrates were given powers to search for and seize arms.

How repressive was Lord Liverpool's government?

A repressive government. The image of Lord Liverpool's government seems to be confirmed by its legislative record:

- The Corn Laws were introduced to protect the interests of landowners, in particular **wheat-growing landlords**.
- Their interests were also served by the much-hated Game Laws of 1815, which introduced the death penalty for the offence of stealing rabbits. The riots in East Anglia in 1816 were partly caused by the economic distress and underemployment of the post-war years but

also because of the tensions which grew out of the issue of poaching.

- Also in 1816 the government repealed the 10 per cent rate of income tax but imposed higher taxes on goods bought by the lower classes such as tea, sugar, tobacco, beer, paper, soap and candles.
- The Six Acts 1819.

A reforming government. Despite the pressures on the Liverpool government, it did manage to suggest and pass some moderate social and financial reforms.

- Without a police force it had to rely on troops, often disorderly yeomanry and panicky magistrates. Few were imprisoned without trial and measures to ban the use of arms and military training can hardly be said to be excessive.
- Despite the timidity and fears of Tory ministers there were modest attempts to address some of the economic grievances of the time. As the economy improved from 1820 onwards, so the number of incidents declined.
- A Factory Act (1816) outlawed the use of children under 9 in cotton factories; insurance was offered to workers in local mines and iron works; and funds were committed to public works in an attempt to reduce local unemployment.
- As political stability was restored and the threat of violent disorder receded, the Tories became confident that more ambitious financial reform could safely be introduced which had been their aim all along. The Wallace Committee (1820) investigated trade reform while the Romilly Committee (1819) advocated far-reaching reform of the legal system.
- There was also important currency reform with the decision by the Currency Commission in 1819 to return to the gold standard which was duly achieved by 1821.

SUMMARY QUESTIONS

1 Why could the period 1815–20 be called 'a period of unrest'?

2 What had the government of Lord Liverpool achieved in domestic politics during the period 1815–22?

3 How did Lord Liverpool's administration balance reform and repression in the period 1815–22?

CHAPTER 3

What was the nature of Liberal Toryism?

LIBERAL TORYISM

Sir Robert Peel, 1788–1850 Peel was the moderniser of the Tory party who renamed it the Conservative Party after the Tamworth Manifesto. A Tory minister 1812–30 and Conservative Prime Minister 1834–5 and 1841–6, he was credited with the foundation of the Metropolitan Police Force and Catholic emancipation. His Tamworth Manifesto of 1834 attempted to abandon Old Toryism and establish a new 'conservative' approach to reforms. He fell from office when two-thirds of his party revolted against his repeal of the Corn Laws in 1846. Peel wanted to protect the institutions of church, crown, aristocracy and Parliament. However, he recognised that reform was quite often the answer to their protection.

William Huskisson, 1770–1830 Liberal Tory and President of the Board of Trade 1823–7, responsible for the abolition of a number of protectionist duties. By the late 1820s Huskisson was a believer in free trade. He became the first victim of the railways when he was killed by a locomotive as he crossed the line to greet Wellington.

After 1821 there was a restructuring of Lord Liverpool's administration that changed the atmosphere of the government. In 1821 Liverpool had experienced a series of defeats in Parliament that raised questions about the credibility of his government. The promotion of younger, more energetic ministers, such as **Robert Peel** as Home Secretary, **William Huskisson** as President of the Board of Trade and Frederick Robinson as Chancellor of the Exchequer, after 1822 gave further impetus to reform initiatives. There was no ideological shift – many of the ideas can be traced to the previous ministers – but greater confidence, expertise and knowledge gave the impression of a more businesslike approach.

TRADE AND THE ECONOMY

A clear example of this was the work of Huskisson and Robinson in reducing the more restrictive elements of the protectionist system.

- In his budgets during the period 1823–5 Robinson reduced the duties on certain imports including silk, wool, coffee and iron. Huskisson attempted to react to the claims of exporters that a strict **protectionist** system damaged their ability to export goods abroad.
- A series of **reciprocity treaties** were signed with a number of European states between 1823 and 1830.
- Huskisson also arranged the relaxation of the **Navigation Acts** with the aim of stimulating Britain's trade with not only its empire but other nations such as the newly independent South American states such as Argentina.
- As Huskisson opened up trade for the benefit of manufacturers, so he made the first move in the

reduction of **protection** for agriculture. However, he was not a fully convinced **free trader** and he recognised the political strength of the landed interests. The compromise was a sliding scale of duties introduced by Huskisson in 1828. The sliding scale reduced the duty on imported corn to a very small amount when the price of corn had reached 73 shillings a quarter. The sliding scale did not signal the end of the Corn Laws but was an important sign that the government was prepared to introduce limited reform to address particular concerns and move towards a *laissez-faire* policy.

THE REFORMS OF PEEL, 1823–30

As part of the reforming nature of the government in the mid-1820s, the Home Secretary Robert Peel introduced various reforms.

- The impetus for such reform had come from the parliamentary committee set up in 1819 under James MacKintosh.
- The Criminal Law Amendment Act of 1826. The aim behind the Act was to simplify, consolidate and improve what was an out-of-date criminal justice system. The Act reduced the number of offences punishable by death by 100. The result was that conviction was more certain.
- Major pieces of legislation passed when Peel resumed the post of Home Secretary and continued to encourage the passage of important reform include the **Juries Act of 1825** and the **Forgery Act, 1830**.
- In 1829 the Metropolitan Police Act heralded the foundation of the Metropolitan Police Force and the reduction of the reliance on informers and troops.
- In his period as Home Secretary, Peel presided over a reduction in the severity of the law. For example, during this time the annual number of public executions fell to 17 from 56.
- Greater controversy was stirred by the Tories' attempts to appease Roman Catholics. The repeal of the Test and Corporation Acts in 1828 allowed the admission of Catholics to Oxford and Cambridge.
- Catholic emancipation. In 1829 Wellington's

Reciprocity treaties Two countries agreed to lower tariffs on each other's goods in an attempt to boost trade.

Navigation Acts Originally passed in the seventeenth century they restricted trade with England (later Britain), demanding that all goods be transported in English (later British) ships.

Protectionism The policy of protecting a country's economy from foreign competition by taxing imports.

Free trade The policy of allowing the import and export of goods without duties.

Juries Act of 1825 This Act regulated the procedure for the formation of juries.

Forgery Act of 1830 This Act retained the death penalty for the forgery of bank notes but reduced the punishment for other forgery-related offences.

government granted Catholic emancipation, thus allowing Catholics to take their seats as MPs. The issue of religious reform is addressed in Chapter 11.

TRADE UNION REFORM

The influence of the French Revolution on politics in the first half of the nineteenth century should not be underestimated. A fear of working-class organisation led to the Combination Acts of 1799 and 1800 which forbade combinations (the union of workers into organisations). However, the Acts were not frequently used, as was shown in 1818 when there was considerable union activity including a strike of cotton spinners in Manchester. Indeed, in 1818 there was an early attempt to set up a general union, i.e. one which included a range of trades. The 1820s saw a change in attitudes towards worker combinations. The ideas of those such as **Jeremy Bentham** convinced many that the repeal of the Combination Acts would actually lead to a reduction in the number of combinations. This argument was taken up by the radical Francis Place. He convinced the leader of the Select Committee of Enquiry into the Combination Laws, Joseph Hume, that the Combination Acts should be repealed. In 1825 the amending Act legalised combinations although they were still subject to certain restrictions. However, trades unions were now legal and free to bargain and strike.

THE END OF 'TORY' RULE

Measures to curb inflation and relax the Corn Laws were resented by many landed aristocrats in the Tory Party who welcomed inflation as a means of reducing their debts and who still believed that their farming income demanded protection from foreign wheat. When Lord Liverpool retired in 1827 the Tories found it difficult to find a leader of such tact and stature, a requirement to maintain party unity. **George Canning**, who succeeded Liverpool, was intelligent and dynamic but was deeply mistrusted by so-called Ultra Tories (see page 12) because of his 'liberal'

Jeremy Bentham, 1748–1832 A writer and philosopher who developed the idea of 'utilitarianism'. This centred around the belief in 'the greatest happiness of the greatest number'. All government policy should be directed to the aim of removing obstacles which would prevent this 'greater happiness' being achieved. Bentham attacked the abuses and weaknesses of existing administration and he strongly influenced the reform of criminal law and the new Poor Law system of 1834.

George Canning, 1770–1827 Tory Foreign Minister 1807–9 and 1822–7, and Prime Minister April–August 1827. As an ex-Whig he became a Liberal Tory, supporting a progressive policy of moderate Tory reform.

foreign policy and his pro-Catholic sympathies. Within a year he was replaced by **Viscount Goderich** who lacked respect and leadership and who resigned in January 1828. The **Duke of Wellington** emerged to restore Tory nerves but dismayed the Ultras by his concession of Catholic emancipation.

SUMMARY QUESTIONS

1 Describe the Liberal Tory reforms in the period 1822–9.

2 Explain the importance of Robert Peel and William Huskisson in the 1820s.

Viscount Goderich (formerly Frederick Robinson), 1782–1859 Tory Chancellor of the Exchequer 1823–1827, and briefly Prime Minister August 1827–January 1828.

Duke of Wellington, 1769–1852 Tory MP and commander-in-chief of the British forces at the battle of Waterloo (1815). Became a minister in 1819 and was Prime Minister from 1828 to 1832 and briefly in 1834. Won a reputation as the 'Iron Duke' and became the idol of early Victorian England.

CHAPTER 4

What were the key features of British foreign policy, 1815–41?

Congress of Vienna, 1815
The representatives from Europe's leading nations met in Vienna to decide the nature of post-war Europe. Austria was represented by its conservative Chancellor Metternich, Russia by Emperor Alexander I and Prussia by King Frederick William III. The Congress of Vienna attempted to restore the status quo of before the wars. The monarchies of Austria and Prussia were restored. Measures to maintain the peace settlements were agreed upon by the leading powers.

KEY FACT

The Quadruple Alliance
Signed in November 1815 by the four leading powers of Britain, Austria, Russia and Prussia after the Congress of Vienna. They agreed to:

- prevent the return of Napoleon and his dynasty,
- preserve the Congress of Vienna settlement,
- protect Europe against any further French aggression.

KEY ISSUE

Castlereagh's priorities at Vienna Castlereagh claimed: 'it is not our aim to collect trophies but to try, if we can, to bring the world back to peaceful habits'.

FOREIGN POLICY AND LORD LIVERPOOL'S MINISTRY

The Napoleonic wars were brought to an end at the **Congress of Vienna** in June 1815. At the Congress Britain was represented by Foreign Minister Viscount Castlereagh and the Duke of Wellington. When Castlereagh became Foreign Secretary in 1814 Britain had been at war with France for 21 years. He played an important role in organising the **Quadruple Alliance** which finally defeated France in 1815. Although he had a cold character, Castlereagh won the respect of the other diplomats during and after the Congress of Vienna for his energy, intelligence and fine grasp of detail.

At the Congress of Vienna, Castlereagh maintained what had been the traditional values of British foreign policy:

- protection of the balance of power in continental Europe to prevent any one power dominating the Channel coastline,
- a policy of non-involvement in European affairs,
- the maintenance of Britain's economic interests and naval supremacy.

THE CONGRESS OF VIENNA, 1815

Britain's leading role in the defeat of France gave it dominant status during the Congress. **Castlereagh's priorities** were to achieve a lasting peace and 'equilibrium' – a balance of power which would deter future aggression by one state. This was of interest to Britain which did not want to be dragged into continental wars.

Most important to Castlereagh was a diplomatic order which would prevent the spread of revolution. Therefore at Vienna he supported the restoration of the Austrian and Prussian monarchies. Like all members of Europe's ruling classes Castlereagh had been horrified by the upheaval and violence of French revolution and he believed that social order and political stability could only be safeguarded by restoring the monarchy in these countries. Castelreagh believed that the two great challenges to this traditional system – **liberalism** and **nationalism** – were 'evils' which had to be contained.

Different attitudes at Vienna

Castlereagh opposed any settlement which would be too harsh on France and would unsettle the country. The monarchy had been restored in France in 1814 after Napoleon had fled to Elba: King Louis XVIII was placed on the French throne. However, there were disagreements among the allies over how the French should be treated.

- It was Castlereagh's aim that the French monarchy remain secure. However, Castlereagh was also determined to ensure that Europe was secure against French aggression.
- Prussia and Russia wanted to punish France for the Napoleonic wars. Tsar Alexander I wanted Russia to be given territories in eastern Europe. Prussia claimed territory in the German states of central Europe.
- The three **autocratic** monarchies of Austria, Prussia and Russia wanted to defend themselves and the status quo by crushing all liberal and nationalist movements.

The Act of the Congress of Vienna was a compromise between these conflicting interests:

- France kept its pre-war frontiers but was forced to accept an army of occupation. It was also expected to pay for the war: a figure for reparations was set at 700 million francs by the Second Peace of Paris in November 1815.
- Austria was strengthened by being given the former Italian provinces of Lombardy and Venetia. It also received Salzburg, Tyrol and Galicia.

KEY THEMES

Liberalism This was the philosophy of those who believed in favouring individual liberty, free trade and reform.

Nationalism The belief in self-determination for nationalities, of a similar language, culture and identity, through the creation of sovereign nation-states.

KEY TERM

Autocratic An autocratic system of government is one which is dominated by an individual with absolute powers.

Changes in Europe after the Congress of Vienna, 1815.

Key

‑‑‑‑‑‑‑‑ State boundaries established in 1815

[illustration] Extent of French Empire in 1812

——— Boundaries of German Confederation

- Although Prussia had to give land to other countries – for example it lost part of Poland to Russia – it was compensated with part of the Grand Duchy of Warsaw (Posen) and Danzig.
- Russia received the former Grand Duchy of Poland which now became a Polish kingdom with the Russian Tsar as its king. Russia also gained part of Finland from Sweden.
- Britain kept Malta, Heligoland and some Dutch colonies including Ceylon (now Sri Lanka) and the Cape of Good Hope.
- The German Confederation was formed to take the place of the Holy Roman Empire. It was to be made up of 39 states.

- Sweden kept Norway which it had gained from Denmark by the Treaty of Kiel in 1814. However, Norway was to be given a separate constitution.

During the Congress of Vienna the leading powers of Europe had agreed that there was a need for them to meet again to discuss further disputes and maintain the peace settlements. In November the four leading powers (Britain, Austria, Russia and Prussia) signed the Quadruple Alliance. The terms of this alliance were very much influenced by Castlereagh's diplomacy. He insisted that the allies agreed to meet periodically to discuss the problems of Europe. This idea of 'government by conference', a '**Congress System**', was accepted.

THE CONGRESS SYSTEM

The issue of intervention

At the first of these conference meetings, the Congress of Aix-la-Chapelle in September 1818, the allies agreed to withdraw their army of occupation from France. Castlereagh played an important role at the Congress in successfully opposing Russian attempts to draw France into a Grand Alliance. At the Congresses of Troppau and Laibach in 1820–1 differences emerged between Castlereagh and those representing the countries of the Holy Alliance (Austria, Russia and Prussia). The most significant cause of tension was the policy of intervention in the internal affairs of other states. Castlereagh shared the fears of the conservative leaders of Europe of radical political movements. He supported the repressive **Carlsbad Decrees** created by Metternich in 1819. However, he was strongly opposed to the great powers coming together to interfere in the affairs of other states. In the **State Paper of May 1820** Castlereagh outlined Britain's policy of non-intervention.

The Spanish revolt, 1820

In the early 1820s revolts in **Spain** and Portugal were both successful in changing the political system. Russia in particular wanted to intervene to restore the Spanish and Portuguese monarchies. The Congress at Troppau met to

KEY TERM

Congress System This was so-called because is was based on the series of meetings that were to take place.

KEY FACT

Carlsbad Decrees, 1819
Devised by Metternich, the Carlsbad Decrees were passed by the *Diet* (Parliament) of the German Confederation in September 1819. They introduced censorship, close control of the universities and an investigation into secret societies. The Carlsbad Decrees controlled German society for a generation.

KEY THEME

State Paper of May 1820
In it Castlereagh wrote: 'we shall be found in our place when actual danger menaces the system of Europe: but this country will not act upon abstract and speculative principles of precaution'.

KEY EVENT

Spanish revolt In January 1820 Colonel Rafael Rigo led a revolt, marched on Madrid and provoked the barracks there to mutiny. The revolutionaries captured King Ferdinand VII and kept him virtually a prisoner until 1823.

consider the situation in Spain. However, in July 1820 a revolt in Naples broke out which had been inspired by the Spanish revolt. As a result, the Neopolitan King Ferdinand I was forced to grant a constitution which concerned the conservative Metternich and his allies. The great powers were persuaded to accept the Troppau Protocol.

- This stated the opposition of Russia, Prussia and Austria to any revolution in Europe which might break up the established order.
- Austria was given a mandate to intervene in Italy, which it duly did. An army marched into Naples in March 1821, overthrew the revolutionary government and restored Ferdinand I.

Castlereagh refused to attend the Congress at Troppau and Britain objected to the Troppau Protocol. This difference in view marked the first serious weakness in the Congress System. However, Castlereagh sent his half-brother Lord Stewart when the Congress reconvened at Laibach in 1821.

Congress of Verona, 1822

In March 1821 a Greek revolutionary society led by Alexander Hypsilanti rose against Turkish rule and appealed for aid from the Russian Tsar Alexander I to assert **Greek independence**. Castlereagh and Metternich were both frightened of such movements and put pressure on the Tsar not to intervene. On 12 August 1822 Castlereagh committed suicide. He was succeeded by **George Canning** who went to the Congress of Verona as British Foreign Minister. However, the Greek revolt was not the only issue which preoccupied the new British Foreign Minister. Canning was determined to prevent intervention in Spain because he feared that such intervention might spread to Spanish colonies overseas. However, after much discussion, the Congress of Verona gave France the permission to crush the Spanish revolt despite Canning's protests. In the spring of 1823 a French army crossed into Spain. By August it had crushed the Spanish revolt and had restored Ferdinand VII to the Spanish throne. Canning's refusal to co-operate further with the other powers in Europe brought an end to the Congress System.

KEY THEME

Greek independence
Hypsilanti had been encouraged in his actions by a member of the Russian government, Count Capo d'Istria. This is why he turned to Alexander I for support.

KEY PERSON

George Canning He shared Castlereagh's opposition to intervention in the affairs of another state.

RELATIONS WITH THE UNITED STATES OF AMERICA

Since the turn of the century, tension remained strong between Britain and the United States of America. There were a number of reasons for the tension:

- *Naval blockades.* In 1806–7 the British and French issued a series of blockade orders which restricted American trade. Tension was heightened by Britain's policy of searching neutral ships. In June 1807 the American ship *Chesapeake* was fired on by the British ship *Leopard* and four deserters were taken from it. Britain, however, needed American military supplies, especially in 1812 when it was fighting the Peninsular War in Spain. Britain lifted its embargo against the United States in 1812 but this move failed to significantly reduce tension between the two countries.
- *Native American opposition.* In the American frontier, American settlers met strong Indian opposition. In 1811 a battle at Tippecanoe was fought between native Americans led by Tenskwatawa and white frontier settlers. Many Americans believed that British aid had strengthened the native Americans militarily and calls were made in the American media for war with Britain and the conquest of Canada.

War with the United States, 1812

War broke out between Britain and the United States in 1812 and lasted for two years. During the war the British managed to burn down much of Washington DC – the US capital. However, Castlereagh recognised the political and commercial **need for a close and friendly relationship with the United States of America**. In 1814 he abandoned Britain's policy of searching all neutral shipping.

The Treaty of Ghent of December 1814 formally brought the war to a close:

- The pre-war status quo was restored by the treaty: neither side lost land.
- A commission was set up to determine the boundary between the United States and British Canada in the disputed northwest.

KEY THEME

Need for a close and friendly relationship with the USA In 1814 Castlereagh wrote: 'There are no two states whose friendly relations are of more practical value to each other or whose hostility so inevitably entails upon both the most serious mischiefs.'

Improved relations after 1817

In the years following the Treaty of Ghent, relations between Britain and the United States of America improved. In April 1817 the Rush–Bagot agreement between the two countries limited naval forces on the Great Lakes. This was followed by a convention in 1818 which established the 49th parallel as the boundary between Canada and the United States from the Lakes of the Woods to the Rocky Mountains. The extent to which Castlereagh was determined to maintain good relations with the United States can be seen in his response to the execution of two British subjects by American forces for taking part in the **Florida raids**. Castlereagh ignored the anti-American hysteria whipped up in Britain and continued to follow a friendly line towards the Americans. Relations were further improved with Castlereagh's opposition to Spanish and Portuguese attempts to restore their colonial role in South America.

Florida raids In 1817 Florida was owned by Spain. However, the United States invaded Florida in 1817 after growing frustration that it had become a haven for smuggling and escaped slaves. It was during the war that followed – known as the Seminole War – that the two British subjects were executed.

GEORGE CANNING AS FOREIGN SECRETARY, 1822–7

George Canning continued many of the policies of Castlereagh. However, he was:

- less sympathetic to the interests of the other powers of Europe;
- more willing to stress the difference between the 'liberal' powers – i.e. Britain – and the 'conservative' powers – i.e. the rest;
- unable to prevent French intervention in Spain in 1823 but he had a significant impact on diplomatic affairs in the next four years.

Portugal

A new constitution for Portugal was drawn up in 1822. It declared Portugal to be a constitutional monarchy similar to Spain and Britain. This was accepted by King John VI of Portugal. However, opposition to a constitutional monarchy came from John's son Dom Miguel. In 1826 he became regent for his niece Maria who had been made Queen. Dom Miguel attempted to change the constitution to make Portugal an absolute monarchy. In that he had the support of France. Canning feared French involvement in Portuguese affairs and in January 1827 sent a naval squadron to Portugal. The intervention was successful. The French did not intervene and Dom Miguel promised to respect the Portuguese constitution.

Latin America

The Napoleonic wars had an important effect on the countries of Latin America. In 1808 Napoleon invaded Spain and put his brother Joseph on the throne. Many of Spain's Latin American colonies took the opportunity to declare themselves independent: forces loyal to the deposed Spanish King Ferdinand VII managed to crush all revolts apart from that in Buenos Aires. However, from 1816 to 1825 a series of wars of independence saw countries such as Chile (1818) and Peru (1821) break ties with Spain. The conservative powers of Europe including France and Russia disliked the idea of republics being formed and the collapse of colonial authority. French intervention in Spain in 1823 and the restoration of the Spanish monarchy led to the threat of European intervention in Latin America and the crushing of the new republics. Canning made it clear that he would oppose any attempt at similar interference in Spain's former colonies. In 1823 Canning attempted to persuade the United States of America to issue a joint declaration warning against any interference in South America by European powers. The American President James Monroe and his advisers did not trust Canning. They feared British involvement in the Americas. As a result the United States issued a declaration against European colonies in the Americas which became known as the **Monroe Doctrine**.

The Eastern Question

In the nineteenth century the power of the **Ottoman Empire** declined and Russia in particular threatened to expand into the Balkans. This posed a serious threat to British interests. Most worrying for Britain was a growth in Russian influence which would threaten Britain's overland route to India and naval position in the Mediterranean Sea. A crisis arose with the declaration of Greek independence from Turkey in 1822. It was in Britain's

South America, showing the independent states and the extent of colonial involvement.

interests to support Turkey but public opinion was strongly pro-Greek. Canning played a complex but successful diplomatic game. He did not want to undermine Turkey and give Russia greater influence, nor did he want to destroy Greek national hopes. Therefore he took the following steps:

- In the face of Turkish attacks Canning allowed the Greeks to put themselves under British protection in July 1826.
- Canning persuaded the Russians to act with Britain. By the St Petersburg Protocol of 1826, Russia agreed to join Britain in mediating between Greece and Turkey. Canning's plan was for Greece to be granted autonomy (self-rule) but with Turkey still having overall authority.

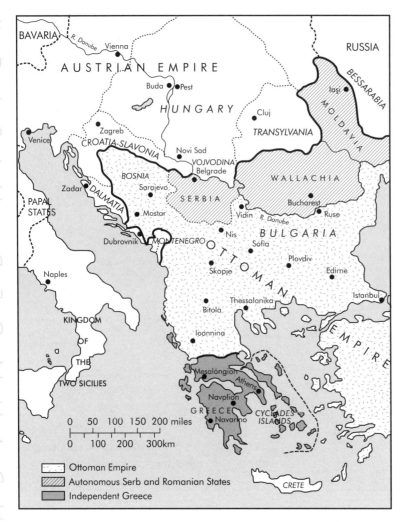

The Ottoman Empire in the nineteenth century.

The Treaty of London of 1827 confirmed this settlement. The Turks refused the treaty. The response of the British, French and Russian navies was to destroy the Turkish fleet at the battle of Navarino. Soon after, in 1827, Canning died.

For the next two years foreign policy was dictated by the Duke of Wellington whose aim was to reduce Britain's diplomatic commitment.

PALMERSTON AS FOREIGN SECRETARY, 1830–41

Palmerston. In 1830 Henry Temple, 3rd Viscount Palmerston was appointed Foreign Secretary by Prime

Henry Temple, 3rd Viscount Palmerston.

Minister Lord Grey. On taking office, Palmerston clarified his main foreign policy objective, that of protecting British interests in the world. Throughout his time as Foreign Secretary he used British sea power effectively as a tool of diplomacy, a tactic which became known as **gunboat diplomacy**. However, Palmerston was a keen supporter of **constitutional regimes**. He welcomed the fall of Charles X in France in 1830 and his replacement by the constitutional monarchy of Louis Philippe. Palmerston was faced with a Europe in which the 1815 settlement was becoming seriously strained. Therefore, he followed a policy of attempting to maintain that settlement.

Belgian revolt

At the Congress of Vienna, Belgium and Holland were united in order to create a country of some strength on France's borders. The new Kingdom of the Netherlands as it was known was not popular in Belgium. Many Belgians disliked any form of political unity with the Dutch. In August 1830 a revolt in Belgium led to a declaration of independence. By the terms of the Congress of Vienna, the King of the Netherlands, William I, should have been supported by Britain and the other leading European powers. However, Palmerston had sympathies with the Belgian cause. At the London Conference which met in June 1831 to resolve the issue of Belgium's independence, Palmerston negotiated the Eighteen Articles which gave Belgium what it wanted. This settlement was not recognised by the Dutch who promptly invaded Belgium. With British help the Dutch were eventually removed from Belgian soil and in 1839 King William finally accepted the settlement: the **Treaty of London** was signed, recognising Belgium as an 'independent and perpetually neutral state'. Palmerston was the dominant figure in the creation of an independent Belgium. He was primarily concerned with preventing the spread of French influence and avoiding war. However, he was lucky in that the Russians were preoccupied with a Polish revolt in 1830 and the Austrians were distracted by affairs in Italy, giving Palmerston a free hand to sort out Belgian affairs.

The Near East

The problem facing Palmerston was the declining power of the Ottoman Empire and the growing influence of Russia in the **Near East**. This was such a concern because Russian influence in that area could affect the route to India. In 1832 an argument blew up between the empire's ruler, the Sultan, and his vassal, the ruler of Egypt, Mehmet Ali, over the issue of who should control Syria. The issue remained unresolved and Mehmet Ali sent an invading force into Syria. By June 1832 Damascus had been captured. The Sultan appealed to the British for help but Palmerston was preoccupied with events in Belgium. He also did not recognise the seriousness of the situation. At the battle of Koniah in December 1832, Mehmet Ali's army defeated the army of the Sultan. In desperation, the Sultan turned to the Russians for help. The Russian Tsar Nicholas I was only too willing to help and sent a squadron of ships to Constantinople. By the Treaty of Unkiar Skelessi in 1833 Russia gained considerable influence in the Near East in return for promising to support the Sultan over the next eight years. This was a diplomatic setback for Britain and France whose policy in the Near East was aimed at limiting Russian power there.

British interests in the Near East. This episode convinced Palmerston of the need for the British to act to support the Sultan whenever necessary. The British ambassador in Constantinople was given the power to summon the British fleet to defend the interests of the Sultan. He was also supported by a trade treaty signed between Britain and Turkey in 1838 which reduced tariffs on Turkish goods. The Near East was of the utmost strategic importance to the British. In 1835 Captain Francis Chesney explored a possible line of communication down the Syrian coast. However, Mehmet Ali rejected British schemes for a railway from Cairo to the Red Sea. As a result the British occupied Aden in January 1839. Palmerston recognised the threat posed to British interests by Mehmet Ali's ambitions. The French, however, built closer relations with the Egyptian leader. In 1839 Mehmet Ali's forces again invaded Syria, defeating the Sultan's forces in the process. To make matters worse, the Turkish fleet sailed to Alexandria and surrendered to Mehmet Ali.

KEY TERM

Near East is the term used to describe the area from the Balkans to Egypt, Syria and Palestine.

KEY TERM

The great powers The victorious countries in 1815. These were Britain, Austria, Russia and Prussia. By the 1830s France was also seen as a great power.

Further success for Palmerston. In July 1839 the Sultan Mahmud II died, to be replaced by Abdul Mehmet who was a mere boy. Abdul Mehmet was prepared to give ground to Mehmet Ali and make him hereditary ruler of Egypt and his principal military commander, Ibrahim, ruler of Syria. At this point the **great powers** stepped in. On the initiative of Metternich a diplomatic note was sent to the new Sultan stressing that the great powers reserved the right to negotiate with Mehmet Ali. However, the French views were very different to those of Britain and Austria. The French supported Mehmet Ali with the hope of increasing their influence in the Near East. The response of Palmerston was to act independently of the French. In July 1840 the Treaty of London was signed between Britain, Austria, Prussia and Russia. Its main points were as follows:

- Mehmet Ali was to be offered Egypt as a hereditary possession and southern Syria for life.
- He was to return the Turkish fleet and give up Crete and the rest of Syria.
- Failure to accept these terms within ten days meant the withdrawal of the offer of southern Syria.

The terms of the treaty were rejected by Mehmet Ali who hoped for French support. There was considerable fury in Paris at being isolated on the issue. The British-led forces bombed Beirut and Acre forcing the withdrawal of Mehmet Ali's forces from Syria. By the Convention of Alexandria of November 1840 Mehmet Ali abandoned claims to Syria. The Straits Convention of July 1841 marked France's return to the five-power fold with the agreement that the Straits were to be closed to foreign warships in time of peace.

Palmerston's Near East policy: success or failure?
Success. There is little doubt that bringing the powers of Austria, Russia and Prussia to the diplomatic table in London in 1840 was a diplomatic triumph. Despite the setback in the early 1830s, Palmerston managed to prevent Russian power growing and he managed to isolate the French. The gunboat diplomacy which brought Mehmet Ali to agreement in 1840 was a trademark of Palmerston's

diplomatic style. It ensured that the Ottoman Empire survived.

Failure. Although the Ottoman Empire survived, the agreement in 1839–40 did not herald a fundamental change. The Ottoman Empire did not attempt any reform and remained the 'sick old man of Europe'. Russia agreed in 1839 to give up privileges in Constantinople but in the long term Russia remained a threat in the region. By going behind France's back in 1839, Palmerston damaged relations between Britain and France.

SUMMARY QUESTIONS

1 How successful was Castlereagh in securing an effective peace 1815–22?

2 How effectively did Canning and Palmerston secure British interests 1822–41?

CHAPTER 5

Why was the political system reformed in the 1830s?

THE CASE FOR REFORM

The concession of Catholic emancipation (see pages 93–6) not only intensified Tory divisions but also encouraged the expectation of reform of the electoral system. Many believed that, if the Tories were prepared to give way on the issue of the Catholics, so they would agree to reform the political system. The electoral system was flawed and in need of reform.

- Only a small number voted.
- There was no uniform **franchise**. This meant that in some constituencies voters had to own a freehold worth 40 shillings a year. In other boroughs (close boroughs) voters had to be a member of the local council. In some boroughs, the majority of men did have the vote, for example Westminster: these constituencies were the exception rather than the rule. Seats were not distributed according to population.
- The growth in population and the emergence of industry simply increased the feelings of inequality. The growing industrial cities such as Manchester, Leeds and Birmingham were not represented in Parliament.
- In the **pocket and rotten boroughs** such as Old Sarum, Dunwich and Gretton, MPs were returned by the patron, there being no voters. In other seats such as East and West Looe the number of voters was extremely small.
- This does not mean that Parliament was completely unrepresentative. In the eighteenth century there was interaction between patrons and constituents. However, this relationship was central to the accusations of corruption.

Tory attitudes to political reform

Apart from the controversial question of Catholic emancipation, the Tories had only been prepared to accept practical commercial and administrative reform. However, Liberal Tories such as Huskisson favoured some kind of gradual change. Most obvious targets for the supporters of reform were the constituencies such as East Retford which were clearly corrupt. **Huskissonite Tories** hoped to transfer the seats to areas where the Members of Parliament would be elected by a larger portion of the population. In 1828 the government attempted a compromise by suggesting that the seat of East Retford be transferred to a nearby area that was under the patronage of the Duke of Newcastle. This idea upset Huskisson and other Liberal Tories who resigned from government over the issue in May 1828. This episode shows how there were tensions within the Tory Party in the latter part of the 1830s over the issue of reform. The Whigs made significant gains in the **election of 1830**. The Duke of Wellington's die-hard defence of the existing constitution in November 1830 led to the downfall of his government and the end of the Tory domination of Parliament. There is no doubt that Wellington misread the mood of the country. He also ignored a section of his own party who wanted reform in order to conserve.

THE WHIGS IN POWER

Led by **Earl Grey** the Whigs formed a government in 1830, which was committed to parliamentary reform. Their coming to power was a crucial step on the road to reform. Although the Tory government had been weakened by internal divisions over reform and Catholic emancipation, it is unlikely that social unrest would have forced a Tory government to reform. The Whigs had been in opposition since 1784 in which time reform of the electoral system had not taken place despite the obvious weaknesses of the system. Both parties had recognised that the old unreformed electoral system was defective.

However, reform had not taken place for a number of reasons:

- The French Revolution of 1789 made those in government worried about making any changes.
- The Napóleonic wars of 1793–1815 and post-war unrest also meant that any attempts at reform were unlikely. Pressure for reform increased as political and economic stability were restored in the late 1820s.

Industrialisation and urbanisation continued to highlight the failure of the electoral system to reflect social changes. In July 1830 news reached Britain of the **revolution in France** which had swept away King Charles X and replaced him with the constitutional monarchy of Louis Philippe. This further encouraged the demands for parliamentary reform in Britain.

Social and economic unrest

It is important to consider the economic context to the campaign for reform during the period 1829–32. In 1829 the harvest was poor and bread prices rose. In 1830 Wellington's government reduced the taxes on a range of goods including beer and malt. The most serious unrest was manifested in the **Swing Riots** which swept the southern and eastern counties in 1830–1. These riots were the result of worsening rural unemployment, the introduction of mechanisation in agriculture, a reduction in the level of poor relief in some counties and the economic distress caused by poor harvests. Although the Swing Riots were not part of any campaign for reform,

KEY TERM

Swing Riots The riots of agricultural labourers in the south of England in 1830 were led by the mythical 'Captain Swing'.

A Swing riot: labourers burn a hay rick in Kent.

they added to the atmosphere of political crisis. In industrial areas, the worsening economic conditions did lead to a revival in the campaign for the reform of Parliament. An example of such a phenomenon was the National Union of the Working Class founded in April 1831. In the general election of 1830, 'Orator' Hunt was elected MP for Preston after campaigning on a platform of reform.

The involvement of the middle classes

One of the most important features of the campaign for reform in the late 1820s and early 1830s was the involvement of the middle classes. Much of their campaigning energy was channelled through the political unions. Inspired by the success of **Daniel O'Connell**'s Catholic Association in winning Catholic emancipation in 1829, about 100 political unions were established to rally support in favour of reform. For two years these well-organised and well-financed groups mobilised and skilfully directed pressure on the Whigs. One of the most successful political unions was the **Birmingham Political Union** (BPU) set up by **Thomas Attwood** in 1829. BPU meetings attracted crowds of up to 100,000 and inspired others around the country to set up similar organisations. In London Francis Place set up the National Political Union. Demonstrations in London were often large; in December 1830 over 10,000 workers met in the centre of the capital to call for an extension to the franchise.

Support from the press

The case for reform was backed by the press. Newspapers in both London and the provinces waged a relentless and powerful campaign in favour of reform. They included:

- the *Two Penny Trash* and the popular *Poor Man's Guardian*;
- national newspapers such as the Whig *Morning Chronicle* which promoted change and provoked Whig leaders into proposing change;
- powerful and influential provincial newspapers such as the *Birmingham Journal* and the *Manchester Times* which provided important support for the campaigns of the political unions.

KEY PEOPLE

Daniel O'Connell, 1775–1847 Catholic Irish agitator who founded the Catholic Association. His election in 1828 led to the granting of Catholic emancipation in 1829. He then led the repeal movement which aimed to abolish the Act of Union with England.

Thomas Attwood A banker from Birmingham. Although he was heavily involved in campaigning for reform of the electoral system he did not believe in universal suffrage. Instead, he believed the vote should be given to the middle classes who would then represent the views of the workers.

KEY ORGANISATION

Birmingham Political Union Its aim was to press for currency reform but Attwood argued that this would not come about until there had been some kind of political reform.

The position of Lord Grey

Lord Grey, the new Whig Prime Minister, argued that the electoral system should reflect the economic contribution now made by the manufacturing and professional classes. It should be stressed that Grey's objective was not to surrender aristocratic control of government, but indeed to strengthen it by allying it to the moderate, respectable and articulate middle classes. The Grey administration was made up of Whigs but also Huskinssonite Liberal Tories such as Palmerston and Goderich and even Ultra Tories. By the autumn of 1830 there was growing pressure on the Whig government to carry out its promise of wholesale rather than limited parliamentary reform. The proposals of the Whigs were primarily aimed at increasing representation of the middle classes in the new industrial cities.

THE WHIG PROPOSALS FOR REFORM

The Reform Bill, introduced by its leading champion Lord John Russell in March 1831, was surprisingly radical. Russell hoped to satisfy radical opinion and provide a 'final settlement' of the constitutional question. It proposed the following:

- a lowering of the property qualification in order to extend the vote to about 300,000 new voters or about 18 per cent of the adult male population;
- all those who owned a house which was rated at £10 a year to receive the vote;
- a redistribution of seats from many boroughs to the growing towns and cities; 168 rotten boroughs would lose their MPs, to be replaced by 43 new borough seats.

In September the Bill was passed in the Commons by one vote but was defeated in the Lords.

Opposition to reform, 1831

The Tories vigorously opposed the Bill, claiming that it would undermine the power of the House of Lords. However, the Tories were divided over the need for reform. Some, such as Robert Peel, accepted that some reform was necessary. However, they rejected the extent of reform proposed by the Whigs. The Tories in the House of Lords led by the Duke of Wellington rejected the idea of reform entirely. Yet Tory opposition in the House of Commons was undermined by the victories of pro-reformers in the **general election in April 1831**.

Popular Protest. In September 1831 a new Reform Bill was introduced into the House of Commons. Again it was passed by the House of Commons, this time with a majority of 109. The House of Lords threw out the Bill. By now the mood in the country was at fever pitch. News of the Lords' opposition prompted **violence** in Derby and Bristol. Those accused of being 'borough mongers', such as the Duke of Newcastle, were threatened. When news of the Lords' rejection of the Bill reached Nottingham, an angry mob attacked and burned down Nottingham Castle which was the property of the Duke.

Tension rises. In March 1832 the House of Commons passed a revised Reform Bill. With the country in a state of unrest, Earl Grey advised the King to appoint enough new peers to the House of Lords to see the Bill passed. William IV was reluctant to create more pro-reform peers and Grey resigned in May 1832. The King then asked the Duke of Wellington to form a ministry. This prospect appalled agitators such as Francis Place who called for a **run on the banks** and Thomas Attwood argued for a national uprising to prevent Wellington's return. It is unlikely that force would have been used by middle-class radicals such as Attwood and Place. However, calls to fight for reform worried Wellington and the King just as they stirred the supporters of reform – both middle and working classes. The **gathering of the unions** in May 1832 was a reflection of the intensity of the campaign.

THE REFORM ACT, 1832

In reality the violence of May 1832 was not as extensive as it had been in October 1831. Along with the pressure from without, reform came about after changes within Parliament:

Gathering of the unions
The meeting of political unions took place in Birmingham on 7 May 1832 with the purpose of persuading the Lords to pass the Bill.

- Unable to form a ministry, Wellington advised the King to recall Grey with the authority, if required, to create sympathetic peers. This the King did.
- Instead of having to introduce new peers, the King persuaded the objecting Tory peers to allow the Bill to pass. In the face of this threat the Lords conceded and the Bill became the Great Reform Act in June 1832.

The significance of the Reform Act

Despite the unrest and pressure on Parliament, the extension of the franchise was limited. The Whigs did not attempt to create a new political system; the new electoral system was similar to the old:

The Great Reform Act of 1832

1 Main qualifications for the franchise in England
   (a) In county seats:
   - adult males owning freehold property worth at least 40s (£2) per annum;
   - adult males in possession of land worth at least £10 per annum;
   - adult males who lease or rent land worth at least £50 per annum (Chandos amendment).
   (b) In borough seats:
   - adult males owning or occupying property worth at least £10 per annum provided they had been in possession of their property for at least one year and were not in receipt of poor relief;
   - existing voters retained that right provided they lived in or within seven miles of the borough in which they voted.
   (c) All voters had to be registered.

2 Changes in the distribution of seats in England
   - 56 boroughs lost their MPs;
   - 30 boroughs lost one of their two members;
   - 22 new boroughs given two MPs;
   - 20 new boroughs given one MP;
   - 64 new county MPs.

- The old political parties – the Whigs and the Tories – maintained their dominance over the system. Some constituencies were still dominated by the patrons such as the Duke of Newcastle.
- Under the old system around 40 per cent of constituencies actually held elections. This figure rose to just under 75 per cent in the December 1832 election.
- Under the new electoral system, those who had previously had the right to vote kept this right for their lifetime. However, as they died out the number of voters in certain constituencies actually fell: for example the electorate in Preston was around 5300 in 1832 but only 2000 in 1857.
- The working classes had not been given the vote and there was no indication of any further reform. It was the Whigs who benefited most from the 1832 Reform Act. In the new House of Commons they held over 500 of the 658 seats. The years which followed reform saw legislation ranging from the Poor Law Amendment Act of 1834 to the Municipal Corporations Act of 1835. This legislation offended many radicals who had campaigned for reform.
- Despite reform the practices of bribery and corruption remained. There were still rotten boroughs and inequalities in representation.

Municipal Corporations Act of 1835

In 1833 the new Whig government ordered a Royal Commission of Enquiry into the state of municipal government, namely the old corporations. Because the Test and Corporations Acts had, until 1828, generally kept dissenters out of local government, the corporations tended to be dominated by Tories. The Commission of Enquiry was led by a Whig, John Blackstone. The Commission report delivered in April 1835 painted the corporations as corrupt, closed and antiquated bodies. As a result, the Whig government proposed a far-reaching reform which was as damaging to the Tories at a local level as the Reform Act had been at a national level.

The main features of the reform:

- A uniform plan for local government was set out for England and Wales. Over 200 old corporations were abolished, to be replaced by 179 elected borough councils. The borough boundaries were to be clearly drawn and lists of voters made. These councils had to present properly audited accounts and raise rates for the payment of a police force. The provisions of the Act did not apply to London.
- The borough councils were to consist of a mayor, aldermen and councillors who were to be elected by the local ratepayers. In practice this did not produce a radical change in the style of local government, a Tory clique often being removed to be replaced by a Whig one.
- The mayor was to be chosen every year by the councillors of the town.

The impact of the reform of local government was not as far-reaching as many had hoped:

- Towns were not incorporated automatically. In many towns and cities there was a fierce political battle before towns requested a charter and became incorporated. This was because those who had controlled the town before 1835 were often unwilling to give up political power so easily. Burnley, which was an important cotton manufacturing town, is a very good example in that it was not incorporated until 1861.
- Incorporation of towns did not mean automatic physical improvement. The new town and city councils had very little power to improve sanitation, paving or the physical environment generally.

SUMMARY QUESTIONS

1 What are the main reasons for the passing of the Great Reform Act in 1832? Explain your answer fully.

2 What were the limitations of the new Act?

CHAPTER 6

What was the extent of factory and mines reform, 1802–51?

PRESSURE FOR FACTORY REFORM

The case for factory reform was presented over a long period of time. Of particular concern to many was the exploitation of children in the new factories. Long hours, harsh discipline and precious little education reflected a brutal system of employment. Often those employed were **apprentices**, born of difficult circumstances.

Pressure for reform came from various groups with their own reasons:

Religion. Often the most active campaigners in favour of reform were those connected to religious groups. The most notable **Evangelical** involved was **Lord Ashley**. But they did not have a monopoly on objections to the exploitation of the factory system.

Political. There were those who opposed the factories because they felt socially threatened by them. This group included landowners who feared loss of political powers to the new class of industrialists. One of the most famous campaigners in favour of factory reform was Richard Oastler. A Tory and an Anglican, Oastler was to play a significant role in bringing the plight of the factory children to public attention. In October 1830 **Oastler's letter to the *Leeds Mercury*** drew comparisons between the conditions in the mills in the West Riding and slavery on the plantations in the United States of America.

Medical. The tradition of medical objections to the conditions in the new factories was strong; the work of Dr James Kay is an example.

With such concerns and arguments in mind, there were limited attempts to restrict the extent of the exploitation of children who worked in the factories.

1802 Act for the Preservation of the Health and Morals of Apprentices

In 1802 Robert Peel (father of the later Prime Minister), introduced a Bill in the House of Commons which became the Act for the Preservation of the Health and Morals of Apprentices. Peel's motives were to prevent the worst excesses of the system rather than limit the influence of the factory owners. The Act provided for the following:

- Children were limited to twelve hours of factory work a day (not taking meal times into account). They were not allowed to work night hours.
- Children were to receive religious instruction and other education.
- Local Justices of the Peace had the power to appoint visitors to factories to ensure that the new law was properly implemented.

However, the 1802 Act was widely ignored. Its provisions were aimed at protecting pauper apprentices but the result of the Act was that they were phased out, to be replaced by supposedly 'free labour'. **Opposition to the 1802 Act** continued and the exploitation of child labour remained; in 1815 a Royal Commission was set up to report on the effectiveness of the 1802 Act.

Factory Act of 1819

The result of the Commission's report was the Factory Act of 1819. The main points of this act were as follows:

- Children under 9 were forbidden to work in cotton factories.
- Children between the ages of 9 and 16 were not allowed to work more than a twelve-hour day.

But again the Act failed to introduce an inspectorate which had the power to enforce its provisions. Similarly, it was difficult for magistrates to prove the age of the children employed as there was no compulsory registration of births. The Act was amended in 1825 with the result that working hours on Saturday were shortened.

THE ARGUMENTS FOR FURTHER REFORM

The arguments for and against further reform of the factory system divided both the political world and the manufacturers.

Reformers

Those in favour of reducing working hours further took a **paternalistic** and **philanthropic** view. Richard Oastler pointed to the degrading aspect of the factory system. He was supported by some manufacturers such as John Wood and Matthew Thompson of Bradford and John Hornby and William Kenworthy of Blackburn. In many manufacturing towns 'short-time' committees were set up to campaign for proposals such as those of **Lord Morpeth and Sir John Hobhouse** in 1831. The campaign was joined by **Michael Sadler**, MP for Newark. Some newspapers such as the Tory *Leeds Intelligencer* and the radical *Patriot* argued strongly in favour of reform. Supporters of factory reform published a large number of books and periodicals showing the evils of the factory system. These works included *The Curse of the Factory System* (1836) by leading reformer John Fielden and *The Evils of the Factory System* (1837) by medical expert Charles Wing.

Opponents of reform

The opposition to factory reform came primarily from mill owners who argued that a reduction in working hours would reduce their profitability. They also argued that cutting the hours of children would lead to the reduction in wages of those who were most needy. Their cause was led by those such as John Marshall of Leeds and James Ackroyd of Halifax and championed by the editor of the *Leeds Mercury*, Edward Baines, and other Whig newspapers including the *Manchester Guardian*. Opposition to factory reform was well represented in the Parliament elected in 1832, for example the MP for Leeds, John Marshall, and the MP for Halifax, John Wood. They were supported by many in the new Whig cabinet who believed in *laissez-faire*

KEY TERMS

Paternalism Treating people in a fatherly way.

Philanthropy Doing things to improve the lives of other people.

KEY THEME

Proposals of Lord Morpeth and Sir John Hobhouse In 1831 they attempted to have the hours of children limited to eleven and a half a day, with proper meal breaks. These proposals were attacked by mill owners in Parliament and the final Act was a mere shadow of the original proposals. Night work was abolished but precious little else achieved.

KEY PERSON

Michael Sadler A linen merchant and initially MP for Newark then Aldburgh, a pocket borough. A fierce opponent of the excesses of the factory system, Sadler waged a campaign in Parliament in favour of factory reform. He lost his seat after the passing of the Great Reform Act in 1832.

and were bolstered by the campaign of the Association of Master Manufacturers.

THE CAMPAIGN FOR FACTORY REFORM, 1832–3

Sadler's Committee

In the wake of the undermining of Hobhouse's Bill, the campaign for factory reform intensified. Michael Sadler attempted to introduce a Bill limiting the working hours of children; this was then referred to a select committee which took evidence from a cross-section of those involved in the factory system. The select committee was chaired by Sadler and took statements from a number of witnesses. Sadler's campaign in Parliament was backed up by a nationwide campaign co-ordinated by Richard Oastler. During Easter 1832 large rallies were held in favour of 'ten hours' in York. Committees were formed in Yorkshire and Lancashire to promote the cause. However, the **Ten-Hour movement** suffered a setback in 1832 when, in the wake of the Reform Act, Michael Sadler lost his parliamentary seat.

Factory Act of 1833

Sadler was replaced as the leading figure in the campaign for factory reform by Lord Ashley, the Earl of Shaftesbury. In April 1833 a **Royal Commission** was set up on the suggestion of one of the manufacturers' supporters in Parliament, Wilson Patten. Those who supported factory reform feared that the commissioners were sympathetic to the mill owners' cause. Wherever they went, the commissioners were given a hostile reception by supporters of the Ten-Hour movement, for example in June 1833 in Huddersfield. The Commission's report found that the factory children worked long hours with little education and they rejected the employers' claims that the children were free agents. The result of the Commission's findings was the 1833 Factory Act. The campaign to restrict all under-18-year-olds to ten hours a day failed.

The main provisions of the Act were as follows:

- Children aged 9–14 were restricted to eight hours work a day with two hours of compulsory education.

KEY THEME

Ten-Hour movement The aim of the Ten-Hour movement was to bring about the reduction in the number of hours worked by adults in all industries.

KEY EVENT

The Royal Commission Commission members included Benthamites such as Edwin Chadwick. Their sympathy with the rules of political economy led to the fear of many in favour of reform that their campaign would be rejected.

- Those under 18 years old were restricted to twelve hours work a day.
- Four inspectors were to be appointed, each to be paid £1000 a year and to be supported by eight sub-inspectors. The introduction of an inspectorate was an important innovation as, for the first time, the Act included provision for enforcement. The issue of the inspectorate went further than factory reform: to many who opposed reform, its creation was an infringement on the civil liberties of the factory owners. It was also seen as a challenge to those who believed in *laissez faire*.

The Factory Act of 1844

The 1833 Factory Act failed to introduce a maximum of ten hours a day for children despite the strength of the campaign in favour. The return of a Conservative government in 1841 raised the hopes of campaigners that a reduction in hours would be introduced. Leading campaigners in favour of factory reform such as Oastler had been Tories. Sir Robert Peel and his Home Secretary **Sir James Graham** did not share such reformist views. However, they took office against the background of an economic slump and serious social disorder. In 1842 the Plug riots reflected the desperation of factory workers at falling wages and seasonal unemployment. Peel was sensitive to the image of his government as oppressive. Indeed, in 1843 Home Secretary Graham introduced a Factory Bill to deal with some of the worst excesses of the factory system. The Bill proposed a reduction in the number of working hours for children up to 13 years old to six and a half hours a day. The education clauses of the Bill – introducing three hours compulsory education a day – raised a storm of protest from groups of **dissenters**. In the spring of 1844 Ashley proposed an amendment to the Factory Bill which would grant ten hours to women and children. The amendment was carried by 179 votes to 170 in committee. In the coming months the Bill failed and a new Factory Bill was introduced. When Ashley attempted to amend this Bill he was heavily defeated by 138 votes.

The Factory Act of 1844 was quite far-reaching in its proposals:

KEY PERSON

Sir James Graham was a very important politician. He was an excellent administrator and a convinced free trader. It was this conviction that had something to do with Peel's conversion to free trade in the 1840s. His administrative skills were seen in his reform of the Navy in the 1830s, his factory reform and his support for Chadwick's public health crusade.

KEY THEME

Dissenters and education
The dissenters believed that compulsory education would strengthen the hand of the Anglican Church in the factory districts. Therefore, they opposed any form of educational provision that was not voluntary.

Factory safety The introduction of safety provisions in factories was due to the large number of industrial accidents. These resulted from the combination of unfenced machinery, tiredness and the close proximity to the machinery that was a feature of working in textile mills. Such accidents were widely reported. An example is this entry from the *Manchester Guardian* written in June 1844, the same month in which Graham's Act became law:

An Oldham girl died after being swung round fifty times in machinery belting, every bone in her body being broken.

- For the first time the Act laid down basic provisions for safety in factories; for example, dangerous machinery had to be fenced.
- Workers injured by unfenced machinery were to be compensated (although magistrates were notoriously reluctant to enforce this part of the law). The 1844 Factory Act was a milestone in factory legislation as it marked the beginning of government interference in the relationship between employer and employee. It was significant that up until 1844 factory legislation had concerned itself with the regulation of child and female labour, as these were the groups that had been seen as vulnerable. The 1844 Act widened the scope of the government intervention.
- The Act asserted that children under the age of 13 should work no more than six and a half hours a day.

Ten hours achieved

The 1844 Factory Act failed to limit working time to ten hours. Peel was an important factor in blocking the Ten-Hour movement. Reform was only possible once he was gone. The campaign for a reduction in the number of working hours was rejuvenated. However, for a time in 1845 the issue was overshadowed by the debate over the repeal of the Corn Laws. When Ashley attempted to introduce a Ten Hour Bill in January 1846 it was swept aside as the question of whether to repeal the Corn Laws reached its climax. When repeal of the Corn Laws was finally introduced, Ashley resigned his seat as a Conservative MP in protest. His successor as leader of the Ten-Hour movement was the MP for Oldham, John Fielden. In a sense a new leader gave the movement new impetus. A new campaign was launched against the background of an economic recession in late 1846. In such circumstances and with the support of journals such as the *Ten Hours Advocate*, launched in 1847, the Bill to secure ten hours was passed in May 1847. Many employers ignored the legislation or attempted to evade it by operating a shift system. Therefore, there was still a campaign to be fought to protect the concessions won in the Act.

The Ten-Hour movement was split:

- On the one hand were those such as Lord Ashley who were prepared to accept some kind of compromise with manufacturers. In 1850 a Bill was introduced in Parliament by Sir George Grey to restrict the number of working hours in a week to 60 and made the relay system illegal.
- Opposed to this compromise were those such as Oastler and Cobbett who argued that this was giving up on the principle of ten hours.

It was not until the 1853 Factory Act that children were granted fixed hours.

CONDITIONS IN THE MINES

It was not just conditions in the factories which caused social reformers concern. The central importance of coal in the new industrial process meant that new mines had been dug and mine shafts were much deeper. However, the coal industry remained virtually unregulated and relied on female and child labour.

Royal Commission. In 1840, after prompting from Lord Shaftesbury, a **Royal Commission** was set up to investigate the conditions of work in the country's mines. Its report in 1842 caused a moral outcry, not only for the fact that it included graphic line drawings. The report showed the brutality of the industry, children as young as four years old working long hours in brutal conditions. The report also showed the dehumanising effect on women of working underground and being forced to undertake heavy labour. It was the intention of Lord Shaftesbury and his supporters to shock society. The report took evidence mainly from those working in family pits where conditions were much worse. In parts of the mining industry, the jobs of hauling were no longer undertaken by women. Indeed, the employment of women underground was increasingly being restricted to south Wales, east Scotland and parts of Lancashire and Yorkshire. To many campaigners it was the moral vacuum in which women and children worked in the pits which was the cause for the greatest concern. Tales of young girls and boys working side by side semi-naked produced particular concern.

KEY THEME

The Royal Commission
The evidence produced in the report described clearly the brutality of the system. Young children would work for twelve hours underground, often without a light, as trappers opening the ventilation doors. Accidents were common.

Children hauling coal past a trapper.

Children descending a shaft on a rope.

Mines Act of 1842

Although the Royal Commission report caused concern, it did not automatically lead to government support for legislation which would interfere with the mining industry. The Home Secretary Graham was sympathetic to the

Mines Bill presented to Parliament by Lord Shaftesbury in 1842. However, the Peel government did not actively support the Bill; nor did it do anything to protect the Bill from mine owners in Parliament, intent on reducing its effectiveness. Despite defeats on detail, Lord Shaftesbury managed to pilot his Bill onto the statute book.

The main features of the Mines Act were as follows:

- Mine owners were forbidden to employ women and girls underground.
- No boy under the age of ten was to be employed underground at all.
- As with the 1833 Factory Act, a **mines inspectorate** was to be provided to ensure that the provisions of the Act were carried out.

KEY ORGANISATION

Mines inspectorate The chief government inspector of mines H.S. Tremenheere was appointed in 1850.

However, the opposition to the Mines Bill during its passage had been intense. In the House of Lords, one of the most powerful mine owners, Lord Londonderry, persuaded his fellow peers to remove from inspectors the power to report on the conditions in the mines, which drastically limited their powers. It was only the series of pit disasters in the late 1840s that persuaded Parliament to pass the Mines Act of 1850. This allowed inspectors to report on conditions in the mines. The 1850 report also made mine owners submit plans to the inspectorate of the workings of their pits. However, despite these steps in the direction of reform, the majority of workers in the mines – i.e. adult males – remained unprotected by legislation.

SUMMARY QUESTIONS

1 Assess the extent of factory reform in the period 1800–51.

2 Explain the motives of those who campaigned in favour of factory reform in the period 1800–51.

3 Assess the role of Lord Shaftesbury in the area of reform of working conditions in the mines.

CHAPTER 7

What were the improvements in education, 1800–51?

Introduction. There were many problems with the education of the young in Britain in the 1830s. The state did not support any system of education. It was the churches, both Anglican and dissenting, which ran the schools which existed. They were fiercely protective of their control over education. The upper classes educated their children at public schools although these schools were in need of reform.

ELEMENTARY EDUCATION 1800

> **KEY TERM**
>
> **Dame schools** These were schools which could be set up anywhere. The person running the school was often an elderly lady, hence their name.

The employment of children in factories and the rapid population rise made the issue of education pressing. In the eighteenth century education for children of the working classes was basic. **Dame schools** and charity schools provided little in terms of a formal education. In 1780 the first Sunday school was set up by Robert Raikes in Gloucester. Raikes proposed the teaching of basic Christian morality, reading and writing to children who otherwise received no formal education. By 1833 around one and a half million students were receiving education in Sunday schools, a figure which had risen to 2 million by 1851. The importance of the Sunday schools was that they provided education for children who were engaged in factory work during the other six days of the week. However, the Sunday schools failed to prevent a fall in the literacy rate during the early nineteenth century. This fall was mainly due to the impact of industrialisation and the demands made on children by the new industrial system. In Preston in the 1750s male literacy stood at 72.7 per cent; this had fallen to 49.6 per cent by the 1820s. Literacy rates improved again as churches, factory owners and the state intervened to provide basic education.

THE ROLE OF THE STATE

The state intervened only indirectly in education. Parliament voted the first state grant of £20,000 for education in 1833; this was raised to £30,000 in 1839. The primary reason for state intervention was concern about the lack of educational provision in the new industrial towns and cities. However, the 1833 decision merely authorised the Treasury to make grants in aid of private subscriptions to build school houses 'for the education of the children of the poorer classes'. The money was granted to two religious societies which ran **National Schools** based on the **monitorial system**. The societies played an important role in extending the provision of elementary education. They also introduced teacher training: in 1839 the Anglican National Society set up a network of colleges to support its elementary schools.

In 1839 it was decided to place the administration of the grant in the hands of the Committee of the Privy Council for Education with **Dr James Kay** as Secretary. He was the first central government education administrator in England. His role was to lay the foundations for the state system of elementary education which was eventually introduced in the 1870s. His work was hampered by **opposition from the churches** in particular. Despite this, Kay's achievements were considerable.

- In 1839 two inspectors of schools were appointed to ensure that the money was well spent.
- Kay ensured that grants were extended to provide for school equipment in 1843 and teacher training in 1846.
- By 1851 there were 17,015 national schools educating 956,000 students.

THE LIMITS TO CHURCH EDUCATION

Despite the improvements introduced by Kay, by 1851 a majority of working-class students were still attending dame schools and other such private institutions rather than National Schools. This was partly because many disliked the religious overtones of the National School system. Also, the National Schools charged a fee of around 1d a week.

Other types of schools were created to deal with those not catered for by the National Schools.

Ragged schools. In 1844 a Portsmouth cobbler, John Pound, set up the Ragged Schools Union. The aim of the union was to provide an education for the poorest children in society. The schools were supported by individuals, including the author Charles Dickens and Lord Shaftesbury. Under their patronage the number of schools grew quickly. By 1852 there were 202 Ragged Schools across the country.

Poor Law schools. Under the provisions of the Poor Law Amendment Act of 1834, boards of guardians were encouraged to set up schools to teach pauper children. Many new workhouses did include a schoolroom but the provision was not as widely adopted as intended. In 1838 the state gave a direct grant to the model pauper school at Norwood but the numbers of students attending pauper schools were not great. This was mainly due to the continuing existence of outdoor relief even after the 1834 Act.

Factory schools. The 1802 and 1833 Acts tried to force factory owners to provide regular education for the children they employed. Some factory owners such as **Robert Owen** at New Lanark and Sir John Guest at Merthyr Tydfil set up factory schools for children in their employment as part of a programme to improve conditions for their workers. The 1833 Act in particular was effectively enforced. However, although factory schools were set up, the standard of education was often poor.

Grammar Schools. The increase in middle class income in the first half of the nineteenth century meant an increase in the demand for private education. This demand was met by grammar schools. Most grammar schools had been set up to provide free education to the poor of a locality. As a result their curriculum was often limited to elementary subjects such as maths and English with some **classics**. However, the first half of the nineteenth century saw the clientele of the grammar schools change. Increasingly the schools depended on those who paid fees, and by 1837 the number of fee-paying students had risen to around two-thirds. As a result, the curriculum of the grammar schools changed to match the demands of the clientele. In 1805 Leeds Grammar School introduced non-classical subjects onto its timetable. These subjects included arithmetic, mathematics, science and even history. Subjects such as business were also taught as the grammar schools increasingly relied on their middle class clientele. The introduction of an examination system in the 1850s and the development of a new breed of head teacher during the same period also stimulated such schools.

Public Schools. Whereas the grammar and endowed schools catered mainly for the middle class, so the public schools educated the aristocracy. These schools continued to teach a curriculum dominated by the classics. In the eighteenth century many of the public schools had mixed fortunes. However, by the first half of the nineteenth century their fortunes had revived due to a number of factors:

- *Change in values.* In the eighteenth century, many public schools had been barbaric. From the 1820s onwards a new breed of headmaster emerged with the aim of transforming the nature of these schools. Perhaps the most famous of these was Thomas Arnold who was appointed as Headmaster of Rugby School in 1828. He soon embarked on a series of reforms at the school, raising the status of the schoolmasters, and improving discipline and morals throughout. Most importantly, Arnold attempted to transform his school into a place where Christian worship was an important part of school life. Arnold's ideas were widely copied and developed by others such as Samuel Butler, who was Headmaster of Shrewsbury school. Despite his reputation, Arnold's reforms were only partly successful, public schools remaining rather brutal establishments, as exemplified in the book *Tom Brown's Schooldays*. However, the image of the schools was transformed and that was most significant in boosting their popularity. Between 1837 and 1869 some 31 boarding schools were set up (such as Lancing in 1848), all of which offered a classical education.

KEY THEME

'Tom Brown's Schooldays' was written by one of Thomas Arnold's students, Thomas Hughes. First published in 1857 it became a best-selling book. It portrays the Rugby School of Arnold's day, stressing the importance of Christianity, and also giving a vivid picture of a schoolboy's life, from fishing and the great cross country race to the rigours of learning Latin verse.

- *Social appeal.* As those involved in industry and business made considerable fortunes, so they began to send their children to public schools in increasing numbers; the factory owner Richard Arkwright, for instance, sent his son to the famous public school, Eton College. As this trend grew, so the numbers of public school educated students entering into the world of business increased.
- *Transport.* The public schools benefited from the improvement in transport which made a national education system possible. The spread of empire also led to a growth in the demand for public school education for the children of those who lived abroad.

Universities. The eighteenth century had seen a decline in universities in England. This matched the stagnation in the institution to which they were so strongly attached – the Church of England. However, the universities slowly embarked on a programme of curriculum reform. A School of Mathematics was introduced at Cambridge University in 1824 to be followed by the introduction of written examinations in 1827. At Oxford University, a separate Mathematics School was created in 1807. This innovation was followed by the creation of schools in law, history and science.

However, despite such changes both Oxford and Cambridge Universities continued to be institutions that primarily served the Church of England. Students would only be admitted to the university if they belonged to the Church of England, a rule that was only relaxed in the 1850s. The vast majority of students came from a gentry, military or clergy background. The fees for a course were high and could only be reduced by the winning of a scholarship. Lectures were poor and hardly ever given and the universities did not seek to reform themselves to the same extent as the public schools during this period.

SUMMARY QUESTIONS

1 Explain the main changes in elementary education in this period.

2 What were the reasons for the improvements in public school education?

CHAPTER 8

How did attitudes towards poverty change in the period 1815–51?

Introduction. The Poor Law was the system used for the upkeep of the poorest members of society. These were generally those who could not afford to look after themselves. As a system designed in the late sixteenth century, it came under terrible strain as population growth, industrialisation and agricultural changes created new problems of cyclical employment and low incomes. The system was not designed for or capable of coping with such problems.

THE OPERATION OF THE OLD POOR LAW

The main features of administration of the Poor Law had been laid out in the Elizabethan Poor Laws of 1567–1601.

The poor received different forms of help depending upon which one of three categories they were put in:

- the 'able-bodied' poor who could not find work and needed work to be provided for them;
- beggars who did not want to work and needed to be punished;
- the 'impotent' poor such as the old or the sick who were looked after in almshouses.

The Poor Law was run at a local level by 15,000 parishes. In each parish a poor rate was raised to pay for poor relief.

Amendments to the system

This system was modified over the years as society changed. The most important changes came from the introduction of enclosure in agriculture and a change in the status and situation of many rural poor. Industrialisation, population growth, cyclical employment and low incomes also created new pressures on the poor

KEY TERM

Outdoor relief was relief given to the poor outside the workhouse.

KEY FACT

Speenhamland system In 1795 the Berkshire Justices' meeting at the Pelican Inn, Speenhamland attempted to find a remedy for the terrible poverty of the agricultural labourers in the county. Their answer to the problem was to supplement wages out of the poor fund. The amount payable was based on the price of a standard loaf of bread and the size of the family in distress. This system was adopted by other, mainly southern, parishes.

relief system. As a result, the Gilbert Act of 1782 allowed for the provision of **outdoor relief** for the unemployed able-bodied and relief in workhouses for the impotent poor.

In the 1780s and 1790s there was distress in many rural areas. The problems were caused by bad harvests, underemployment, low wages and rising food prices. A particular problem in the 1790s was the rise in the price of bread as a result of the Napoleonic wars. The worst hit areas were the south-east and south-west of England, Wales and Scotland. One response by parishes was to subsidise the wages of the hardest hit. Labourers' wages were subsidised in Cambridgeshire from 1785. The best known example of a parish supplementing wages out of the poor system was the **Speenhamland system**, set up in 1795.

The impact of the Napoleonic wars

The end of the Napoleonic wars in 1815 saw agricultural depression which was to have a serious effect on the numbers of poor. After 1815 around 400,000 servicemen returned to Britain looking for work. Inflation and falling wages led to an ever-increasing demand on the poor rate. As a result of an increase in poverty, the amount spent on relieving the poor rose sharply, from £2m in 1784 to £9.3m in 1817–18.

Relief was not just given as allowances to supplement wages:

- **Labour rate.** Under this system a parish rate was raised to cover the cost of looking after the able-bodied unemployed. Employers could then choose either to pay their part of the rate or to employ certain labourers. A wage rate was set for each labourer employed and this figure deducted from the employer's poor rate. The system was used in about 20 per cent of parishes in the south of England before 1832.
- **The Roundsman system** involved able-bodied pauper labourers being employed for different ratepayers of the parish in turn. The ratepayers would pay part of the wages of the poor with the parish paying the rest.

CHANGING ATTITUDES TOWARDS THE COST OF THE POOR

There was a noticeable change in attitudes towards the poor rate in the decade which followed the end of the Napoleonic wars. It was the farming and landowning section of the community which was most vociferous in complaining about the growing burden of the **poor rate**. Between 1802–3 and 1832–3 poor rates rose by 62 per cent. In the same period, the value of farm land rose by only 25 per cent. This relative increase led to friction within rural communities. Often tenant farmers who were expected to pay the poor rates passed on the burden of payment to the landowner by negotiating lower rents. The view of the rural communities that the poor rate burden was growing can be clearly seen in the Parliamentary Committee Reports on the Poor Laws in 1817 and 1818. Good harvests reduced wheat prices considerably. As can be seen in the table opposite, even when poor relief expenditure fell, the price of wheat fell further. It is this relationship between falling prices and high poor relief expenditure which created an atmosphere in the country for a change in how the poor were managed.

Malthus. The growing concerns of the rural ratepayers should be placed in some context. The population of England and Wales rose from 9 to 14 million from the 1810s to the 1830s. Therefore, the amount of poor relief paid per head fell from 12 or 13 shillings to 9 or 10 shillings. However, there was at this time a change in economic and political theory. The influential writer the **Reverend Thomas Malthus** claimed that a growing population would outstrip the food supply and result in famine. Therefore, argued Malthus, relief for the poor on the lines of the Speenhamland system was foolish as it encouraged a growth in the population. According to Malthus the system of allowances encouraged early marriages and large families. In reality the Speenhamland system was in decline by the 1830s. However, this did not stop critics of the system using it to argue that it promoted rather that solved poverty. The census of 1821 showed a 14.72 per cent increase in the population of rural areas between 1811 and 1821.

Poor relief expenditure and wheat prices, 1816–1822

Year	Total poor relief expenditure (£000s)	Wheat prices (s d)	
1816	6911	78	6
1817	7871	96	11
1818	7517	86	3
1819	7330	74	6
1820	6959	67	10
1821	6359	56	1
1822	5773	44	7

(Source: J.D. Marshall, *The Old Poor Law, 1795–1834*, Macmillan, 1985.)

The Poor Law and the political economists

The Poor Law was attacked by the writers of what was known as 'political economy'. One of the most influential writers of this school of thought was **David Ricardo**. He believed:

- The Poor Law should be abolished as it interfered with the laws of economics.
- The giving of poor relief increased public expenditure without any purpose.

Ricardo was not alone; in the *Wealth of Nations*, written earlier in 1776, **Adam Smith** suggested that the Poor Law restricted competition and interfered with the working of the economy by preventing labour moving around the country looking for work.

Perhaps the most important critics of the Poor Law system were the disciples of Jeremy Bentham. Led by Edwin Chadwick and **Nassau Senior**, they argued that the old Poor Law was inefficient and actually encouraged poverty.

Resentment at the levels of the poor rate

The ideas of the political economists provided the context for the political attack on the old Poor Law. As already shown, the landowning rural classes increasingly resented the paying of a poor rate which would lead to the poor being treated with some humanity.

There were examples from across the country of reductions in the poor rate:

- The Cambridgeshire bread scale (which was used to calculate the amount of poor relief paid) had been reduced by 1821 to two-thirds of the 1783 level.
- In Nottinghamshire in 1821–2 'reforms' undertaken by Poor Law administrators Reverend R. Lowe, Reverend J.T. Becher and Sir G. Nicholls aimed to make the system of poor relief far harsher, ending the system of allowances and creating a workhouse as a deterrent to the poor.

Equally important in the minds of politicians and the rural ratepaying classes was the fear that pauperism could lead to crime. In reality it was not the different types of poor relief which encouraged pauperism. Much more important were the low incomes earned by agricultural labourers and the cyclical nature of their employment. The greatest concern of those at the time was **the moral effects of pauperism.**

Swing and the result of unrest

The Swing riots of 1830–1 provided the turning point in attitudes towards the poor. Rioting by agricultural labourers spread across the south of England. In 1830 there were around 1400 reported incidents of rural violence. The government responded with repressive measures. In all around 2000 suspected rioters were arrested; nineteen were executed and approximately 1000 were transported or imprisoned. The level of unrest was interpreted by the new Whig government led by Earl Grey as evidence of the failure of the old Poor Law to adequately deal with rural poverty. In 1832 the government set up the Royal Commission on the Poor Laws headed by the Bishop of London with the task of investigating the administration of the Poor Law and suggesting alterations to it.

THE ROYAL COMMISSION ON THE POOR LAWS, 1832–4

The Commission set about its task by collecting data on the administration of the Poor Law from around the country. Twenty-six assistant commissioners toured the country collecting information on around one-tenth of the parishes which contained approximately one-fifth of the population. However, the 'Answers to Rural Queries' and 'Answers to Urban Queries' were used only selectively by the Commission. The most influential commissioners, Edwin Chadwick and Nassau Senior, believed that it was their duty to 'educate the public'. The information from the 26 assistants was generally ignored as the Commission followed its own ideological agenda. This was based on the following ideas:

Moral effects of pauperism In 1824 the Select Committee on Labourers' Wages pointed out that the worst effect 'is the degradation of the character of the labouring class'.

- the Speenhamland system put the idle and hard-working on the same level;
- **allowances** were harmful to society as a whole and widespread.

The report

The findings of the Poor Law Commission damned the existing system of poor relief.

- The report condemned the Speenhamland system as being wasteful. In particular, it suggested the allowance system actually encouraged a growth in population and ever-increasing pauperism.
- The report quoted the parish of Chelsbury (Buckinghamshire) where the amount collected for the poor rate rose from £10 18s 0d in 1801 to £367 in 1832. Such a figure was unrepresentative of the rise in the poor rate in the vast majority of parishes. This attack has since been shown to be inaccurate by a number of historians.
- The report criticised many of the officials who administered the Poor Law, for example the overseers who collected and distributed Poor Law money.
- The report damned the state of many workhouses which administered **indoor relief**. It reported that in some workhouses paupers spent the day without working whereas in others the sick and lame were herded together with children.
- The Commissioners selectively used the evidence collected for them. The historian M. Blaug has called the report 'wildly unhistorical'. However, the report should be seen in the context of the political philosophy of the day, hence the concentration on able-bodied 'idleness' and economic 'waste'. Indeed M. Blaug has shown that the Speenhamland system was not as widespread as the report suggested. In fact the real problem in the countryside was not the allowance system but unemployment and low wages. Allowances were used not to supplement wages, as the report suggested, but to supplement the income of the family.
- Dr J.P. Huzel has proved that in counties where the Speenhamland system was used, such as Kent, Wiltshire and Berkshire, there was a fall in population in the

period 1815–30. This disproved the claims of the Commission that allowances resulted in a growth in population. Huzel argued that the allowance system was a reaction to low wages not a cause.

THE POOR LAW AMENDMENT ACT OF 1834

The report from the Poor Law Commission was long and detailed. It was drafted by Chadwick and Senior. Their priority was to improve the administration of the Poor Law rather than deal with the issue of the cost of poverty. This factor greatly influenced the nature of the Poor Law Amendment Act of 1834 which was the legislative response to the report. The Poor Law Amendment Act was one of the most significant pieces of legislation of the century. It was both an administrative revolution and marked a significant change in public values.

Administration

The report tried to show that the parish lacked the financial resources and administrative talent to deal with the poor. Therefore, the 15,000 parishes were combined to form 640 **Poor Law Unions** administered by boards of guardians and professional officials. The guardians were to be elected by the ratepayers.

This form of **local** government was to be controlled by a **central** body. The role of the **Poor Law Commission** was to ensure that the Poor Law was administered uniformly across the country. The Commission had three members, the first Secretary being Chadwick. England and Wales were divided into 21 Poor Law districts, each under the control of an assistant commissioner. Their job was to make sure that the boards of guardians carried out the policies and rules of the Poor Law Commission. So, the Poor Law was administered at a central and a local level.

Poor relief

The key theme of the Act was the abolition of outdoor relief which the report had called 'the great source of abuse'. The report had stressed the importance of the moral and economic independence of the labourer. Hence,

Centralisation versus localism The creation of a central body – the Poor Law Commission – with powers to oversee decisions made at a local level provoked considerable friction and debate. The dual approach reflected the ideological divisions in the Commission. The Benthamites as represented by Chadwick or Senior believed in centralisation for administrative reasons.

Poor Law union The main administrative unit of the new Poor Law.

Poor Law Commission It was this central body that so many people objected to, claiming its powers to be excessive and unconstitutional.

under the new system a reduction in the number of paupers could be achieved by insisting that the able-bodied had to be destitute in order to qualify for relief. This relief could only take place in a workhouse. The conditions in the workhouse were to be less attractive or **less eligible** than those suffered by the worst paid workers.

Limitations of the new Poor Law

There were many problems with the new system, many the result of the ideology behind the new Poor Law:

- The new Poor Law had an oversimplified view of poverty. It concentrated far too much on the single issue of the rural able-bodied unemployed. Therefore, the model was not suited to the **poverty in the new northern industrial sector** of the economy.
- In times of a trade depression such as in the late 1830s and early 1840s the workhouse could not cope with the numbers of those temporarily unemployed.
- Many of those who had to administer the new Poor Law resented central interference but also failed to see the relevance of the workhouse to industrial areas. In 1837–8 an Anti-Poor Law movement objecting to the new system was born in Yorkshire mill towns such as Bradford, where there were riots in 1837, and Dewsbury where there was resistance to the new Poor Law in 1838. Politicians such as John Fielden and Richard Oastler attacked the Act.
- In some areas allowances continued to be paid. The workhouse system as suggested by the new Poor Law was not introduced into Lancashire or Yorkshire until the 1860s.

The stigma of poverty

The new Poor Law was very unpopular with the working classes. It politicised individuals such as **Feargus O'Connor** whose involvement with the Anti-Poor Law movement resulted in him searching for a political solution to the Poor Law, i.e. Chartism. The regime in the workhouses was strict as intended by Chadwick. By 1839 around 350 workhouses had been built by local unions.
Contemporaries attacked conditions as inhumane. There were scandals at some workhouses in which paupers were

poorly nourished. In the Andover workhouse in 1845 paupers worked crushing bones to produce fertiliser; an inspection of the workhouse found paupers were keeping bones to gnaw to ease their hunger. Indeed, one problem in implementing the Poor Law was the fact that in the 1840s there were only ten inspectors.

Although the day was strictly regimented and the paupers put to work, in many workhouses the work was not hard. The greatest objection of the poor to the new Poor Law was the dehumanising effect of the workhouse. The separation of married couples and the housing of children separately caused bitter resentment. There was a slight

KEY THEME

Contemporary attitudes In *Oliver Twist* Charles Dickens commented that 'all poor people should have the alternative of being starved by a gradual process in the house [workhouse] or by a quick one out of it'. However, Dickens was probably exaggerating: the diet in many workhouses was basic but sufficient.

A workhouse yard in the 1840s.

relaxation of the rules: in 1847 an Act permitted workhouse authorities to allow married couples over 60 to live together. Otherwise paupers were categorised into groups with different living arrangements, for example the able-bodied men or children under seven. This reinforced the image of the workhouse as a form of 'moral imprisonment' – what *The Times* called the 'new **Bastille**'.

Allowances

In 1835 the first Outdoor Relief Probationary Orders were issued to southern rural unions forbidding outdoor relief to the able-bodied. The only people who could, with the consent of two JPs, claim outdoor relief were the aged and infirm. In 1844 a general Outdoor Relief Prohibitory Order was issued to cover nearly all Poor Law unions. However, the situation was not that simple. Some unions continued to issue outdoor relief. In 1847 the Poor Law Commission was abolished to be replaced by the **Poor Law Board**. In the same year around 26 per cent of unions still issued some form of outdoor relief. One reason why this practice continued was because of necessity; another because many unions found it a cheaper way of dealing with the poor than putting them in workhouses.

Opposition to the Poor Law

Among the working classes opposition came in response to the stigmatisation of poverty. Those forced into the workhouses were classified into different groups, for instance, able-bodied women or children under seven, and were immediately separated thus into different living quarters. Cambridgeshire petitioners protesting against such proposals in 1836 spoke of how they were 'dismayed and disgusted' at the idea. There were outbreaks of violence in Kent in June 1838 which reflected such bitterness against the new law.

The centre of opposition to the new law lay in the industrial north where there was opposition from both working people and some members of the propertied classes. In 1837 the commissioners attempted to form Poor Law unions in the north. The climax to the opposition was the Anti-Poor Law movement which flourished in 1837 and 1838 and thereafter was absorbed into the Chartists.

The movement incorporated many different groups that opposed the Act. The most significant point is that the new law did not suit the patterns of employment common in the new industries. Most obviously, it did not take into account the fact that employment could still be seasonal.

Tories. Many Tories such as **Richard Oastler** believed the new Poor Law to be an attack on the old paternalistic society. They asserted that the new Poor Law would break the bond between rulers and ruled.

Anti-centralisation. Much of the fiercest opposition to the new Poor Law came from those who objected to the centralised authority of the new Poor Law Commission. Many northern parishes had already embarked on a programme of rationalising the old system. As the economy prospered in 1835 and 1836 these parishes experienced a fall in the poor rate. The overseers of the poor in Little Bolton, for instance, claimed a fall in the poor rate in 1835–6 'without the interference of the Poor Law Commission'. To many the powers of the Poor Law Commission were a dangerous infringement of the freedom of localities to organise their own affairs. Therefore the Anti-Poor Law campaign was supported by many influential members of the community such as magistrate John Fielden of Todmorden. As the new Poor Law was designed to meet the needs of the able-bodied rural poor so many argued it was unsuited to the north for the reasons given above. Some magistrates such as those in Huddersfield refused to implement the new system.

Working class opposition. With the economic depression of 1837 the opposition to the new Poor Law 'Bastilles' grew. In Bradford in 1837 and Todmorden and Dewsbury in 1838 there were riots in response to the attempts to introduce the workhouses. The government crushed these riots by sending the Metropolitan Police to the area. The campaign against the new Poor Law was well organised because it fed off the culture of protest of the reform movement and Ten-Hour movement.

In 1837 a South Lancashire Anti-Poor Law Association was founded in Manchester which organised local

Oastler's opposition
Oastler's attitude towards the Poor Law can be summarised by his claim that 'It lays the axe to the root of social compact; it must break up society and make England a wilderness'.

committees in the surrounding factory towns. The movement was well served by support from sections of the press, from the Tory *Leeds Intelligencer* to the radical *Northern Liberator*. Public meetings and large open-air demonstrations were held such as that held on Hartshead Moor in 1837. The response of a concerned government was to advise caution on the part of Boards of Guardians to take the steam out of the protest. To an extent this policy was successful, since much of the working class support for the Anti-Poor Law movement became swallowed up by Chartism.

THE NEW POOR LAW SYSTEM

- Administratively the new Poor Law was a relative success. The unions were successfully created; they built workhouses which operated on a 'less eligibility' principle.
- However, the Poor Law Commission could not impose the new system over the whole country immediately. Many of the aspects of the old Poor Law continued, especially in the north. These included the practice of giving outdoor relief.
- The new Poor Law failed to solve the problem of pauperism. Although there was a reduction in the numbers of those who claimed benefit from 1.26 million in 1834 to 1 million in 1850, the new Poor Law did not deal with the causes of poverty.

SUMMARY QUESTIONS

1 'The Poor Law created more problems than it solved.' Do you agree or disagree with this statement?

2 What were the aims of those who framed the Poor Law Amendment Act of 1834 and how far did they achieve their aims?

CHAPTER 9

How were public health problems tackled, 1830–51?

THE IMPACT OF INDUSTRIALISATION

Industrialisation led to a rapid growth in the size of Britain's towns and cities. In the 1820s alone, some of the major cities nearly doubled in size, for example Liverpool and Manchester grew by 46 per cent. Immigration from Ireland in the 1840s further boosted the urban population. Although housing was built to cater for some of this increase, it was not enough. The pressure of population on many urban districts was immense, for example the parish of West Derby in Liverpool experienced a population rise of 140,000 between 1801 and 1851. Overcrowding became the norm with families sharing the most basic of

This ilustration entitled 'A Court for King Cholera' shows the conditions in which the disease could rapidly spread.

facilities. **Common lodging houses** were an excellent breeding ground for disease with their overcrowding. In London in 1854 there were 10,824 lodging houses with 80,000 inhabitants. In some cities people lived in cellars, for example around 20 per cent of the population of Liverpool in 1840. These cellars were poorly ventilated and damp.

SANITATION

The lack of sanitation was a particular problem. In many of the larger cities sewage heaps of up to 35,000 tons built up in the middle of densely populated areas. Provisions for dealing with the appalling conditions found in a number of cities were often haphazard and inadequate. Despite improvements made after the Municipal Corporations Act of 1835, many towns had several organisations dealing with different aspects of the problem, for example highway committees, improvement commissions and paving trusts.

Disease

The result was disease on an epidemic scale. In October 1831 **cholera** broke out in Sunderland and spread across the country killing 32,000. Another cholera epidemic in 1849 claimed 53,000 victims. The causes of cholera were not known although the medical establishment linked the poor sanitary conditions to the outbreak of disease. The most popular theory for explaining disease was the **miasmatic theory**. In response to the cholera of 1831, a central Board of Health was set up with local boards of health across the country.

Their main tasks were to:

- respond to any complaints about poor drainage and other public health related issues;
- appoint inspectors whose task was to report on the state of public health in their locality.

The Cholera Act of 1832 gave the local health boards the authority to fund anti-cholera activity from the poor rates. Given the widespread objection to state intervention this Act was a significant move.

Cholera was by no means the only problem. Typhus killed large numbers in 1837, 1839 and 1847. Smallpox, diphtheria and measles killed large numbers at regular intervals. Disease provoked concern from numerous quarters, the medical profession in particular. In 1831 **Dr Charles Turner Thackrah** and in 1832 Dr James Kay undertook studies of urban areas and the impact of disease. Their work was greatly helped by the creation of statistical societies such as the Manchester Statistical Society which undertook extensive research into conditions in different parts of the country. From 1837 all births, deaths and marriages had to be registered. The new Registrar General William Farr insisted that, as part of the procedure for the registration of deaths, the cause of death be given.

EDWIN CHADWICK

The introduction of the new Poor Law had important effect on the investigation into public health. The leading campaigner for reform was Edwin Chadwick. A Poor Law Commissioner, Chadwick was concerned with the link between disease and poverty.

Chadwick was a convinced Benthamite:

- He believed that public health conditions placed unnatural obstacles in the way of the poor seeking work and happiness.
- On a more down-to-earth level, disease and a high mortality rate placed a strain on the poor rate.

Edwin Chadwick.

Chadwick's Benthamism was reflected in many of the administrative solutions he suggested to deal with the problems.

In 1838 Chadwick wrote to the Home Secretary Lord John Russell stating the view of the Poor Law Commissioners that poor public health conditions were placing a significant burden on the poor rate. A Commission of Enquiry was set up to look at the problem. The three Commissioners, Neil Arnott, James Kay and **Thomas Southwood Smith** were Benthamites like

Chadwick but also had a real interest in public health affairs. In the process of accumulating information, the Commissioners visited some of the worst areas of London. Their report stated clearly that disease was linked to poor sanitation, overcrowding and bad water. For the first time a government report had highlighted the need for preventive measures to be taken to improve the living conditions of the poorest in society. It was followed in 1840 by a Select Committee on the Health of Towns, led by Robert Aglionby Slaney. The **Health of Towns Commission** produced reports in 1844 and 1845.

REPORT ON THE SANITARY CONDITION OF THE LABOURING POPULATION OF GREAT BRITAIN

The most significant contribution to the public health debate was the *Report on the Sanitary Condition of the Labouring Population of Great Britain* published in 1842. In 1839 the Bishop of London Dr Blomfield proposed in the House of Lords that a survey be undertaken of the levels of disease throughout England and Wales. In 1840 the scope of the enquiry was widened to include Scotland. The enquiry was to be led by Chadwick whose methods of investigation and proposals for centralised authority provoked considerable opposition. In the end the report had to be published in Chadwick's name alone and publication was delayed until 1842. The opposition arose for various reasons:

- **Chadwick's personality.** Chadwick was a most direct and humourless individual. His tendency to lecture made him many enemies both inside and outside Parliament. His most severe critic was John Walter, editor of *The Times*. As a member of the Poor Law Commission he was well known for his bullying tactics. Chadwick was also quick to show contempt for even potential allies. In 1841 the Whig government introduced three Bills to improve public health. Chadwick poured scorn on these Bills as not going far enough. In his report Chadwick alienated other Commissioners by attacking a range of interests from the medical profession to the London water companies.

KEY ORGANISATION

Health of Towns Commission Its reports recommended improvements in sewerage and drinking water and greater powers for local authorities.

KEY THEME

'The Report on the Sanitary Condition of the Labouring Population' came in three volumes. The first two volumes consisted of the reports from the different regions of Great Britain. These had been compiled by a range of interests including the medical profession and Poor Law officials. The third volume was Chadwick's own reflections and findings.

- **Localism.** Despite the obvious need for some form of central co-ordination, many jealously protected the right of local authorities to choose what they felt was the best course of action for their areas.

The report itself very much reflected Chadwick's view of the important issues relating to public health. Its conclusions were as follows:

- The whole issue of public health needed to be addressed. 'The annual loss from filth is greater than the loss from death or wounds in any wars in which the country has been engaged in modern times.'
- Poor conditions created poverty and the poor should not be blamed for the conditions in which they lived.
- Parliament should insist on improved water supplies which were necessary for better sanitation.
- Medical officers were needed.
- Refuse should be removed from where people lived by an efficient sewerage system.

Campaign for reform

The findings of Chadwick's report and those of the Health of Towns Commission were at first ignored. In 1844 Chadwick played a leading role in the creation of the **Health of Towns Association**. The aim of the association was to lobby for public health legislation and reform. Its tactics were, in a sense, similar to those of the Anti-Corn Law League. Meetings were held and information widely distributed through the *Weekly Sheet of Facts and Figures*. Minor reforms were passed, including the Town Improvement Clauses Act and the Waterworks Clauses Act both of 1847 and both of which attempted to encourage local authorities to take measures to improve public heath.

PUBLIC HEALTH ACT OF 1848

In 1848 the Whig Home Secretary Lord Morpeth introduced the Bill for Promoting the Public Health. The Bill represented an uneasy compromise between those such as Chadwick who wished for compulsion from the centre and his opponents who believed that local initiative was

KEY ORGANISATION

The Health of Towns Association The association was particularly effective in raising awareness of public health issues. Its slogan, 'the heaviest municipal tax is the fever tax', was directed at those who feared that public health improvement would lead to an increase in taxation.

more important. When passed into law the Act made the following provisions.

- A **General Board of Health** was set up in London with some compulsory powers. However, its scope was limited because the Act was permissive. That meant that the General Board of Health could suggest various courses of action but had no power to force the local boards or authorities to act when they did not want to do so. Another shortcoming of the Act was that it did not apply either to Scotland or London. Public health in London remained in the hands of over 300 authorities.
- Local boards of health could be set up in places where the death rate reached or was greater than 23 deaths for every 1000 people.
- Medical officers were to be appointed by these boards to oversee public heath issues.

The new legislation came into effect in 1848, at the same time as a new cholera epidemic broke out. However, opposition against the main provisions of the Act continued. Although by 1853 the Act had been applied in 182 towns, many local authorities resisted introducing local boards of health. In 1854 the General Board of Health was dissolved and Chadwick sacked.

Opposition

Opposition to public health reform was in part due to ignorance of the causes of diseases such as cholera and was in part ideological. Both strands of opposition were further stimulated by Chadwick's somewhat arrogant attitude. *The Times* newspaper had a long-standing campaign against Chadwick fearing the centralisation that he proposed in his 1842 report. Chadwick was convinced that the answer to the problems of public health lay in centralising administration and better engineering. However, he still believed in the 'miasma' theory that disease was carried in the air. Until Dr John Snow proved in the 1850s that the cholera germ was carried in water, ignorance of the causes of the disease meant that many objected to Chadwick's proposals.

SUMMARY QUESTIONS

1 How significant was Chadwick's contribution to public health reform?

2 What were the obstacles to public health reform during the period 1830–51?

CHAPTER 10

What was Chartism?

Introduction. The Chartists were one of the most extraordinary phenomena of the period. They were so called because of their adherence to the six point manifesto of what they called The Charter. This exclusively political programme won support from many suffering economic hardship.

BACKGROUND TO CHARTISM

The origins of Chartism lay in the mixture of **political frustration** and **economic hardship**. The Chartist movement was highly complex and diverse. It was a radical movement. Its roots lay in the development of English radicalism of the late eighteenth century and the writings of those such as Thomas Paine and John Cartwright. Their importance was in the idea that society's problems could be solved by **parliamentary reform**. This belief was shown in the campaign for reform in 1830–2. The campaigners for reform relied on working-class support which was readily given. However, when the Great Reform Act was passed, the suffrage was not extended to include the working classes. This was to be of great importance in the development of Chartism.

The reform campaign provided many lessons for those who wanted political change thereafter; in particular the belief that unrest could provoke change, for example, the May unrest of 1832 was seen by many as intimidating Parliament into passing the Great Reform Act.

The nature of the legislation which was passed by the Whig-dominated Parliament in the 1830s encouraged working-class support for political change. The most obvious piece of legislation which had this effect was the new Poor Law of 1834. It was this Act with its workhouses and its harsh treatment of the poor which fuelled grievances about the political system.

KEY THEMES

Political frustration The limited nature of the Great Reform Act of 1832 excluded the working classes.

Economic hardship The result of the economic slumps of the 1830s and 1840s which were related to bad harvests and weak demand for manufactured goods.

Parliamentary reform Crucial to an understanding of Chartism. The aims of the Chartists were to push for reform, out of which would come an improvement in living and working conditions.

THE WAR OF THE UNSTAMPED

As part of the Six Acts of 1819, the government imposed a stamp duty (a kind of tax) on newspapers. This included weekly journals and magazines of the type written and circulated by radicals such as William Cobbett. The aim of the government was clear: it would use the stamp duty to close down all radical journals by making them unaffordable for the working classes. In the 1830s the duty was challenged by working-class radicals such as William Lovett, James Watson and, most importantly, Henry Hetherington. In 1830 the publisher John Docherty produced cheap unstamped papers. In London Hetherington published the *Poor Man's Guardian* which achieved a readership of over 16,000. Despite the attempts of the government to suppress the unstamped newspapers, they continued to publish. Between 1831 and 1836 around 740 sellers of unstamped newspapers were prosecuted. In the end, however, the government gave in. In 1834 the *Poor Man's Guardian* was declared legal by a court. The following year the stamp duty was lowered to 1d by Lord Melbourne's government, making all newspapers affordable.

Consequences of the war of the unstamped

There were far-reaching consequences of the struggle to lower the stamp on newspapers:

- The newspaper the *Northern Star*, which was at the heart of the Chartist movement, emerged from the battle. Many of those who were to work on the *Northern Star*, including its editor George Harney (who succeeded the Rev. William Hill in the post), had connections with the unstamped press.
- Many radicals who later became Chartists had been involved in the war of the unstamped. They absorbed the lessons of the struggle and used the structure of radical organisations which had been formed. In 1835, for example, a Society for the Promotion of the Repeal of Stamp Duties had been formed. Out of this developed a working-class organisation, the London Working Men's Association (LWMA) founded in 1836,

which was to have a central role in the development of
the Chartist movement.

THE ORIGINS OF CHARTISM

Political origins. Chartism was a response to the political
exclusion of the working classes by the Reform Act of
1832. It was fuelled by claims of those such as William
Lovett that political representation had to be won before
the working classes could ensure economic prosperity. This
helps to explain the explicitly political nature of the
Charter drawn up by Lovett and Francis Place in 1837 and
published in May 1838. It was aimed at a Whig
government whose reforms of the mid-1830s were
perceived to be oppressive, most obvious of all being the
new Poor Law. Yet this is where Chartism was unique.
Whereas the factory reform and ten-hour movements and

The Six Points
OF THE
PEOPLE'S
CHARTER.

1. A VOTE for every man twenty-one years of age, of sound
mind, and not undergoing punishment for crime.

2. THE BALLOT.—To protect the elector in the exercise of
his vote.

3. NO PROPERTY QUALIFICATION for Members of Parliament
— thus enabling the constituencies to return the man of their
choice, be he rich or poor.

4. PAYMENT OF MEMBERS, thus enabling an honest trades-
man, working man, or other person, to serve a constituency,
when taken from his business to attend to the interests of his
country.

5. EQUAL CONSTITUENCIES, securing the same amount of
representation for the same number of electors, instead of
allowing small constituencies to swamp the votes of large
ones.

6. ANNUAL PARLIAMENTS, thus presenting the most
effectual check to bribery and intimidation, since though a
constituency might be bought once in seven years (even with
the ballot), no purse could buy a constituency (under a system
of universal suffrage) in each ensuing twelvemonth; and since
members, when elected for a year only, would not be able to
defy and betray their constituents as now.

The Six Points of the
People's Charter, by
Lovett and Place,
published in 1838.

the **Anti-Poor Law campaign** sought to remedy grievances on a particular issue, the aims of Chartism were more fundamental. To an extent this was its greatest weakness for, to achieve its aims as defined by the Charter, it would have needed a political upheaval the like of which the country had not seen since the seventeenth century.

Economic origins. The origins of Chartism are complex. Yet there is no doubt that the demands for political reform were fuelled by the worsening economic conditions of the late 1830s and early 1840s. To this extent the claim of the Reverend J.R. Stephens that Chartism was a 'knife and fork' question was accurate. The years 1838–9 saw a considerable depression in manufacturing areas which coincided with a rise in support for the Chartist cause. In Nottinghamshire and Leicestershire, for example, support for Chartism was strong among the hand loom knitters who suffered from a decline in trade.

THE EMERGENCE OF CHARTISM, 1837–8

Chartism emerged out of a revival in radical agitation in London and Birmingham. As explained above, the Charter was drawn up in London. It was a product of radical disappointment over the failure of 1832. This helps to explain why the committee formed in 1837 to debate the issue of working-class representation included radical MPs J.A. Roebuck and Colonel Thompson. Yet Chartism was not simply a London phenomenon. In **Birmingham** in 1837 radical MP Thomas Attwood revitalised the Birmingham Political Union (BPU). Initially, Attwood's demands for political change were limited and at odds with the radicals from London. He was not an immediate convert to universal suffrage believing in household suffrage and Parliaments every three years. However, Attwood was converted to the principle of universal suffrage in November 1837. As economic conditions worsened, so the campaign for a national petition gathered momentum. In May 1838 the national petition which became the People's Charter was launched at Glasgow by representatives of the BPU, LWMA and other radical organisations. This was followed by large meetings in

KEY THEME

Anti-Poor Law campaign
One of the reasons for the upsurge of popularity for the cause of the Charter in the late 1830s was the appeal it held for those such as supporters of the Anti-Poor Law movement whose campaign had failed.

KEY CITY

Birmingham was a very important regional centre and a city at the heart of the Industrial Revolution. It was an important centre of engineering. It also gained significance through its position on the canal network which linked it to towns from Walsall to Liverpool. Its economic position gave it political significance.

Birmingham in August and at Kersall Moor outside Manchester in September.

Support for Chartism

Support for the Charter came from around the county. There were many smaller radical movements formed with different emphases. One such example was the Marylebone Radical Association formed in 1835 by Feargus O'Connor but which stood apart from the LWMA because of its **links with the middle classes**. However, O'Connor was wedded to the Charter just like Lovett and Hetherington. It was O'Connor's aim to spread the message of the Charter and in 1837 he founded the *Northern Star* and appointed the Reverend William Hill as its editor. The newspaper

The 'Northern Star'.

flourished in a climate of agitation. In 1837 a large-scale anti-Poor Law demonstration had taken place at Hartshead Moor which the *Northern Star* gleefully reported. However, O'Connor's primary aim was to promote the cause of universal suffrage and the ideas of a national convention and a national petition in support of that cause. At Hunslett Moor in June 1838, O'Connor founded the Great Northern Political Union which differed in tone from the more artisan-based LWMA. In a series of meetings in northern industrial centres in late 1838, O'Connor developed the theme of **physical force** if peaceful means should fail.

THE NATIONAL CONVENTION AND CHARTER, 1839

The National Convention met in London in February 1839. Delegates had been sent from around the country, with the north the best represented with 20 out of the 53 delegates. The Convention was soon embroiled in internal wranglings over tactics, relations with the anti-Corn Law movement and the next steps to take. In particular there were divisions over what to do if the Charter was rejected. The result was that some delegates drifted away, concerned at the increasingly aggressive language of many of the other delegates. In May 1839 the Convention moved to Birmingham. It now considered various points, including a 'sacred month' (general strike) and arming Chartist supporters. Tensions rose throughout the country. Mass meetings were held at Hartshead Moor (21 May) and Kersall Moor (25 May) among others. However, the authorities had begun to act against the Chartists: for example, a prominent Chartist Henry Vincent was arrested and Major-General **Sir Charles Napier** was put in charge of a force of 6000 soldiers based in the north. On 4 July a riot broke out in the Bull Ring, Birmingham, after police were called in to break up a Chartist meeting. The Chartist leadership immediately condemned the actions of the authorities with the result that Lovett was arrested.

On 12 July 1839 the Charter was presented to Parliament. Containing over 1,280,000 signatures it was summarily

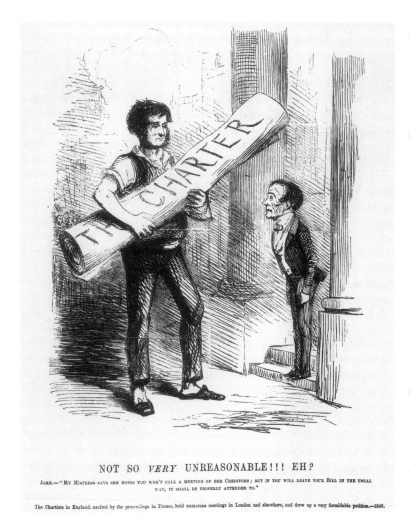

NOT SO *VERY* UNREASONABLE!!! EH?

JOHN.—"MY MISTRESS SAYS SHE HOPES YOU WON'T CALL A MEETING OF HER CREDITORS; BUT IF YOU WILL LEAVE YOUR BILL IN THE USUAL WAY, IT SHALL BE PROPERLY ATTENDED TO."

The Chartists in England, excited by the proceedings in France, held numerous meetings in London and elsewhere, and drew up a very formidable petition.—1848.

An illustration from 'Punch' magazine showing the presentation of the Charter. Note how the magazine seems to be cautiously sympathetic.

rejected by 235 votes to 46. The dilemma for the Chartist leadership was to decide what the next step would be. O'Connor shied away form direct action recognising how badly any uprising would fare. However, events elsewhere now took their course.

The Newport uprising, 1839

In early November 1839 a crowd of around 7000 colliers and ironworkers led by **John Frost** descended on the Welsh town of Newport. The nature of the area's industry and the determination of its workers to see the Charter won by whatever means led to the rising. Newport was defended by a group of soldiers who killed 24 Chartists in the battle for the Westgate Hotel. Of the 21 Chartists committed to trial for high treason, three – including the

---

KEY PERSON

John Frost A linen draper who became a leading Chartist. Frost had not wished for armed agitation, indeed as an ex-magistrate he urged caution on the crowd. However, in the wake of the fiasco Frost was arrested and tried. He spent seventeen years in Australia.

leader, Frost – were sentenced to death. However, the unrest across the country at the beginning of January 1840 convinced the authorities of the sense in commuting the sentences to deportation. What followed effectively ended the first stage of Chartism. In 1840 most of the Chartist leaders including Harney, Lovett and O'Connor were arrested and imprisoned.

THE 1842 CHARTER

Despite the imprisonment of most of its leaders, the Chartist movement survived because of its strength at grass-root level. In July 1840 the **National Charter Association** (NCA) was founded. Despite its growth, support for the NCA was not even countrywide. One problem was its association with O'Connor who, still languishing in York gaol, had given it his blessing. There were few members of the association in either London or Scotland. However, in late 1841 O'Connor was released and this gave impetus to the collection of signatures for another petition and Charter in 1842. Support for the second petition was considerable. This was in part due to the severity of the economic depression of 1842. The Chartists were better organised and the convention which met in April 1842 far more orderly than that of 1839.

The petition that was presented to Parliament in May 1842 by T.S. Duncombe contained over 3 million signatures. Again, Parliament rejected the petition by a large majority. In the summer of 1842 there was a wave of industrial unrest in the north which became known as the Plug riots. The strike and riots in Manchester and other leading industrial centres were not inspired by the NCA or any other central Chartist movement. However, many of the strike leaders had been Chartists and the authorities responded to the violence with another round-up of known Chartists. This was partly in response to the fact that the NCA had backed the strikes. By the end of 1842 around 1500 Chartists had been charged with various offences.

THE DIVERSITY OF CHARTISM

KEY PERSON

William Lovett The key to understanding Lovett is that he stood apart from both the middle classes and industrial workers. His movement was rooted in the political beliefs of the artisans of London; radical and non violent in methods.

William Lovett.

Feargus O'Connor.

Historians have made much of the differences between the 'physical force' approach threatened by Feargus O'Connor and the 'moral force' approach of **William Lovett**. Yet the differences in tactics between Lovett and O'Connor are not clear-cut.

Lovett. While imprisoned in 1841, Lovett wrote the book *Chartism* in which he repeated his commitment to the principles of the Charter. However, Lovett's 'new move' was to argue that education was the key to working-class improvement and Chartist credibility. In 1841 Lovett founded the National Association which was supported by fellow Chartists such as Hetherington; it was an indication of the diversity of Chartism. O'Connor dismissed Lovett's ideas as a distraction.

O'Connor. O'Connor believed that Chartists should arm themselves, but this was not unusual in an age in which bearing arms was common. He believed primarily in parliamentary petitioning as the means by which working-class advancement could be achieved. This was a view shared by the broad base of support the movement enjoyed. Chartism flourished in communities threatened by industrial change, such as the hand loom weavers of Lancashire and Nottinghamshire. One strand of Chartism was rooted in nonconformist religion, especially in Scotland. Led by Arthur O'Neill, Christian Chartist churches attracted working-class adherents happy to mix their faith and politics. By 1842 there were over 20 Chartist churches in Scotland. However, at the centre of the movement remained the Charter. None of the distractions or proposed alliances with other groups meant a compromise of the movement's political demands.

O'CONNOR'S LAND PLAN

After the failure of the Charter in 1842 O'Connor explored further ideas which he felt would empower the working classes. He turned to the question of the land, its ownership and significance. To O'Connor, ownership of land could secure working-class freedom from oppression. In 1845 the Chartist Land Co-operative Company was set up with the purpose of buying land. The idea was that this land would be rented out in two-acre batches for £5 a year to those who had joined the scheme. O'Connor believed that Chartist communities would emerge from this land plan. The scheme was very popular and within three years the co-operative had 70,000 members.

The reasons for its popularity are clear:

- In times of economic hardship, the prospect of escape from underemployment appealed to many.
- The harvest of 1847 was poor across Europe.

The first Chartist community was established near Watford in 1846 and two others at O'Connorville and Lowbands (Worcestershire) in 1847. These were to be followed by three other communities. However, in all only 250 Chartists were actually settled on the land by the plan. The company was eventually wound up by an Act of Parliament in 1851 because of **legal difficulties**.

THE 1848 PETITION

The 1847 general election saw Feargus O'Connor elected as Member of Parliament for Nottingham. The new Whig government led by Lord John Russell was immediately faced with the prospect of economic distress as the result of a poor harvest and the continuing problem of unrest in Ireland. In 1848 revolution in France gave encouragement to those who hoped for some kind of radical rising in Britain. A series of **disturbances in London**, Glasgow and Manchester were linked to Chartism by the popular press. The unrest was not the product of Chartist agitation but more a sign of the serious economic problems of the time. On the back of these problems, support for the Charter grew. O'Connor addressed meetings across the country including one on Kennington Common in front of a crowd of 20,000. A Chartist Convention was called in April 1848 and agreed to the following strategy:

Land plan and legal difficulties Those to be settled on the land were chosen by lot. This meant that the company set up by O'Connor in 1845 could not be registered as a friendly society. Nor was it registered as a joint stock company and therefore it was, technically, illegal.

Disturbances in London In March 1848 a meeting against income tax in Trafalgar Square was taken over by Chartist G.W. Reynolds. The meeting was followed by riots in Trafalgar Square and across London which took three days to end.

The Chartists meeting on Kennington Common.

- A petition was to be presented to Parliament after a mass public meeting.
- If the petition were rejected a national assembly would be summoned which would sit until the Charter was granted by Parliament.

Given the events in France, the government and middle classes reacted with alarm at the proposed events. The procession to Parliament was banned by the police in April. The Duke of Wellington was put in charge of the defence of the capital and 85,000 **special constables** were enrolled. The Queen left London for the Isle of Wight. The meeting duly went ahead on 10 April at Kennington Common. O'Connor spoke to the 20,000-strong crowd advising them that the procession had been forbidden. The petition of some 2 million names was duly presented to Parliament and was promptly rejected. Following the Charter's rejection, an attempt by Ernest Jones was made to set up a national assembly in May 1848. However, Jones's assembly lacked support from other Chartist leaders including O'Connor and it duly dissolved itself.

SUMMARY QUESTIONS

1 What were the main obstacles to the Chartists achieving their aims?

2 What were the strengths and weaknesses of the Chartist movement?

CHAPTER 11

What were the main changes in religion, 1820–51?

Introduction. The first quarter of the nineteenth century witnessed little reform of the established Church of England. There were many injustices connected to religion. The Church of England was supported by a system of taxes which non-Anglicans (for example Catholics or nonconformists) had to pay. This injustice was made worse by the abuses within the Church of England.

POSITION OF THE CHURCH OF ENGLAND 1820.

The Church of England was the **established church** in England and Ireland. In the 1820s the Church maintained its privileged position in society. The lack of church reform in the first two decades of the nineteenth century should partly be put down to the impact of the French Revolution which encouraged conservatism. It is accurate to describe the Church as **Tory in doctrine** and practice. Many of the leading clergy could be described as **high church** in their political and religious views. There was no attempt to challenge ideas and this meant that many of the worst aspects of the Church remained. These were as follows:

- **Pluralism.** A churchman could be in charge of more than one parish. As each parish provided an income, it was a way for churchmen to increase their wealth.
- **Absenteeism.** Vicars could hold parishes and receive payment for their work but did not need to live in or attend the parish.
- **Differences in clerical income between parishes.** While some churchmen were comparatively wealthy, others were not. The result was that the quality of religious provision varied.

KEY ISSUE

Tory in doctrine There were few who wanted to change the Church or how it worked.

KEY TERMS

Established church One which is recognised by the state as being the national church.

High church Those who were high church believed that the Church's property and privileges should be defended.

Dissenter One who belonged to a church other than the Church of England, for example, the Baptist or Quaker churches.

The Church was maintained by rates which were paid by Anglican and **dissenter** alike. Taxes raised by the Church such as that of **First Fruits and Tenths** were highly unpopular. Not only did those who did not belong to the Church have to pay for its upkeep but they were discriminated against in public life. Dissenters were prevented from holding public office by the Test and Corporations Acts. These Test Acts had been passed in the seventeenth century as a way of preventing non-Anglicans from holding public office. All those who did not take the sacrament of the Church of England were legally discriminated against. Because the Church of England was the established church, it received funding directly from the state. In 1819 Lord Liverpool gave the Church a grant of £1m to fund new church building. As a result, in the 1820s alone over 300 new Anglican churches were consecrated.

EVANGELICALISM

The Church of England was a broad church which meant that it embraced many different religious movements. One of the important influential movements was Evangelicalism. This movement emerged in the 1780s and comprised Anglicans who chose to stress the ideas of personal salvation and godliness. Identified with individuals such as John Venn, **William Wilberforce** and Hannah More, the Evangelicals stressed the need for 'vital religion'. Although the number of Evangelicals in the Church of England was not great, they were very influential. The Clapham Sect, which flourished from the 1780s, was the foremost Evangelical group in the country. In the early nineteenth century Evangelical views flourished through religious societies, the most influential being the Church Missionary Society. One of the more notable Evangelicals of the period was Charles Simeon who extended the influence of Evangelicalism at Cambridge.

The impact of Evangelicalism
The impact of Evangelicalism was not just felt on religion:

• Anglican Evangelicals played an important part in a

KEY FACT

First Fruits and Tenths
These taxes had been raised by the Church until Henry VIII's time. He had confiscated them during the Reformation. However, in 1703 they had been restored to the Church as a means for small parishes to sustain themselves.

KEY PERSON

William Wilberforce was closely identified with the campaign to abolish slavery. An Evangelical Christian, he became a leading member of the Clapham Sect. Wilberforce also supported campaigns for factory reform and the improvement in the living conditions of the working class. He also supported the concept of elementary education for all. He died in 1833.

reformation of customs and manners in the early part of the nineteenth century.

- The Clapham Sect played an important role in promoting the abolition of slavery in 1807.
- Campaigning methods used to good effect in the fight to abolish the slave trade were also used by groups such as the Society for the Suppression of Vice. Leading figures in the Evangelical movement after Wilberforce's death included Lord Ashley. Much of Ashley's reforming zeal was inspired by his Evangelical beliefs. This is perhaps the most important effect of Evangelicalism: a generation of reformers were inspired by their religious principles.
- However, Evangelicalism was to have an impact on all classes more directly. An example was the spread of Sabbatarianism, the attempt to set aside Sunday solely for religious observance, advocated by the Society for Promoting Due Observance of the Lord's Day, which was set up in 1831.

REPEAL OF THE TEST AND CORPORATIONS ACTS, 1828

The growth of dissent was an important factor in the drive for the reform of the Anglican Church. Stuck in an eighteenth-century constitution, the Church's position left it open to attack. One such privilege was the Anglican monopoly on public offices. Such a monopoly was, in practice, not upheld. Every year Parliament passed an Indemnity Act that protected dissenters from prosecution. Yet this was the type of law which so damaged the Church of England. In practice the Church gained little advantage from it but it provoked considerable hostility towards the Church from dissenters. In 1827 the United Committee of Dissenters was set up to campaign in Parliament for the repeal of the Test and Corporations Acts. In 1828 Robert Peel as Home Secretary accepted the overwhelming support for repeal of these Acts and the Bill put to Parliament by Lord John Russell became law. However, this was not before Peel insisted on an amendment which stated that dissenting office-holders must promise not to subvert the established church while in office. The repeal of the Test and Corporations Acts was an important symbolic victory for the dissenters as it showed that reform of the established church was possible.

CATHOLIC EMANCIPATION

The issue of **Catholic emancipation** had been an important political one for a considerable amount of time. Although the Church of England was a broad church, it was united by common themes, one of which was **anti-Catholicism**.

The question of emancipation was bound up with a number of issues among which were:

- Ireland, where the majority of the population were Catholics but were held back by the laws such as the remaining Penal Laws that discriminated against Catholics;
- the role of the Church of England as an established church.

The Whigs and emancipation

Catholic emancipation became a central feature for the Whigs. Pitt the Younger had attempted to introduce a form of Catholic emancipation. He believed that emancipation would strengthen the Union between England and Ireland. However, Pitt was thwarted by the **opposition of George III**. Indeed, royal opposition to Catholic emancipation was a common theme, even after George's death and the accession of George IV to the throne. The unpopularity of Catholic emancipation among the wider population could be seen in the 1807 election during which Whigs were heckled with cries of 'no popery'.

The Tories and emancipation

Despite the fact that popular opinion was very much opposed to emancipation, certain enlightened Tories such as Charles Greville and George Canning supported the idea. They did so out of a belief that emancipation would improve the situation in Ireland. The Tories were split on

King as Supreme Governor of the Church of England
In the coronation oath, the monarch swore to uphold the Church of England as its ruler.

Protestant ascendancy was the Protestant dominance of all aspects of Irish life.

Daniel O'Connell.

Daniel O'Connell Known as the 'the Liberator', O'Connell promoted peaceful methods of achieving political change. At the heart of his campaign was demand for Catholic emancipation 'without wing', i.e. without strings attached. O'Connell linked the cause of emancipation to that of Irish nationalism and, thereby, drew the Catholic Church into a nationalist alliance. O'Connell was a populist and an eloquent orator who appealed through the power of his speeches.

the issue, with older Tories such as Lord Liverpool opposing the idea. He was backed by younger Tories such as Robert Peel who believed emancipation was incompatible with Toryism. Their opposition was based on the following principles:

- Emancipation would destroy the constitution and undermine the position of the **King as Supreme Governor of the Church of England**.
- The removal of legal discrimination against Catholics in Ireland would lead to the destruction of the **Protestant ascendancy** and further demands which might lead to the break up of the Union.

Although emancipation Bills passed the House of Commons in 1821 and 1825 they were defeated by the Tory majority in the Lords. This was also the case for Bills which aimed to remove some, but not all, of the discrimination against Catholics, such as Nugent's Bill of 1823.

Daniel O'Connell

In 1829 Catholic emancipation was introduced by a Tory government led by the Duke of Wellington, with Peel as Home Secretary. While Wellington did not have strong ideological opinions, Peel did. However, both became convinced of the need for Catholic emancipation in the light of events in Ireland. In 1823 **Daniel O'Connell** and fellow lawyer Richard Shiel formed the Catholic Association of Ireland. The aim of the association was to achieve emancipation and promote the cause of Irish nationalism. By charging peasants 1d a month for membership – the 'Catholic rent' as it became known – the association grew quickly in terms of popularity and resources. In 1825 the movement was closed down but an alternative, the Order of Liberation, continued to raise money for the cause. The significance of these movements is that they mobilised Catholic opinion successfully in Ireland and in such a way as to raise the profile of the issue of emancipation. In the 1828 general election O'Connell won one of the two Clare seats despite being **barred from actually taking his seat**.

Emancipation is granted

O'Connell's electoral victory in County Clare posed Wellington's government a real dilemma. In 1828 and 1829 there was widespread unrest in the Irish countryside. Such was the momentum behind O'Connell's campaign that Wellington and Peel feared that to further block emancipation would lead to rebellion in Ireland. This is the key to explaining Peel's U-turn on emancipation. In supporting Wellington, Peel received much abuse from Ultra Tories and those who believed that such a measure would herald the end of the established church. However, the introduction of emancipation was not the complete victory suggested by O'Connell's supporters. Peel ensured that the impact of Catholic voters would not be so strongly felt by raising the Irish franchise from a £2 freehold to a £10 freehold.

THE ESTABLISHED CHURCH UNDER ATTACK

At the heart of the campaign for reform of the Church of England was a concerted campaign by dissenters to have some of what they saw as injustices removed.

The repeal of the Test and Corporations Acts in 1828 and Catholic emancipation in 1829 did little to reduce criticism:

- In 1830 the Whigs came into office with many MPs believing in **utilitarianism** and looking to reform the Church. Hostility towards the established church can be seen in pamphlets such as *The Extraordinary Black Book* (1831) which attacked the Church's position.
- The attack on the Church of England did not come solely in print. In 1831 there was a series of physical attacks on the Church which included the burning down of the bishop's palace at Bristol.
- The Reform Act of 1832 strengthened the influence of those who dissented against the Anglican Church and political radicals. Groups such as the United Committee were formed by Presbyterians, Baptists and others with the aim of campaigning for Church reform.

- It was not just dissenters and radicals who pressed for Church reform: Archbishop Howley of Canterbury, for one, believed that the issue had to be properly addressed.
- Even among the Tories, who were the strongest supporters of Church privilege, there were those such as **Robert Peel** who recognised that some element of administrative reform was necessary.

REFORM OF THE CHURCH OF ENGLAND

In response to such pressure, far-reaching reforms of the Church of England were introduced in the 1830s.

The Ecclesiastical Commission

In 1832 an Ecclesiastical Commission was appointed by Lord Grey to review the state of the Church of England and to look into the issue of ecclesiastical revenues in particular. One of **Robert Peel**'s priorities on becoming **Prime Minister** in 1834 was to reduce hostility to the Church by introducing administrative reforms. As one who wished to protect the Anglican Church from attack, Peel recognised the need to remove the most blatant abuses. In February 1835 he gave considerably **greater powers to the Ecclesiastical Commission**. The aim of the Commission was not to attack the Church of England, far from it. Peel wanted the Church to strengthen itself through reform. Therefore, the Commission's membership included not only Peel but two archbishops and three bishops, among others. Although Peel lost office in April 1835 the work of the Commission continued. When the Whigs returned to office they simply replaced Tory members with Whig members and in 1836 they set up the Commission on a permanent basis.

The nature and extent of reform of the Church

The need for reform was obvious and the political recognition of this meant that reform was forthcoming.

- By the Established Church Act of 1836 the income of bishops was standardised at £4000 for all but the most important archbishops. This was of critical importance because income had been unfairly distributed with episcopal income being disproportionately greater than the pay raised at parish level. With the creation of new parishes in industrial areas, such redistribution was long overdue.

- There was another attack on the injustices in Church funding with the Ecclesiastical Duties and Revenues Act of 1840 which further redistributed wealth from cathedral to parish.
- The unpopular **tithe** was reformed in 1836 by the Commutation of Tithes Act.

Despite this legislation the extent of reform was not as far-reaching as many dissenters and their political allies in Parliament had hoped. This was partly due to the inbuilt majority in the House of Lords which was against reform of the Church.

Similarly, the Whigs were only prepared to go so far in reforming the Church for fear of an electoral backlash:

- The Marriage Act of 1836 allowed dissenters to marry in their own chapels but an amendment of the Bill in the House of Lords ensured that they still had to have their marriages announced first by the Poor Law guardians.
- In 1837 an attempt to abolish Church rates failed in the House of Lords and the Irish Church Tithe Bill was undermined by amendments.

THE CHURCH IN IRELAND

The established church in Ireland was the Church of Ireland. Whereas in England there was considerable objection from minorities to paying tithes to support the Anglican Church, the case in Ireland was even stronger. In Ireland the Church of Ireland was the minority church with only 7 per cent of the population as members. Although Peel hoped that Catholic emancipation would help stem the tide of unrest in Ireland this was not the case. In the 1830s Catholics in many areas refused to pay the tithe. The disturbances reached the point that in 1833 a Coercion Act was passed by the new Whig government with the aim of introducing **martial law**. However, Lord Grey also recognised the need for reform of the Irish Church.

KEY TERMS

Tithe A tax amounting to a tenth of one's income which was payable to the Church.

Martial law A country or area is ruled by the armed forces and civil law is suspended.

In 1833 Grey's government introduced the Irish Temporalities Bill:

- The Church of Ireland was to be reorganised with the number of bishoprics reduced.
- Parishes where there were no worshippers should not receive any income.
- Most importantly, the extra money freed up by these reforms should be used for social projects such as the improvement of education. This was too much for the Church establishment on both sides of the Irish Sea, the Tories and even many Whigs. The result was that this part of the Bill was dropped.

Divisions within Whig ranks remained over what to do with the Church of Ireland and especially the issue of excess revenue. Again in 1835 a Bill sponsored by Lord John Russell to reform Irish Church finances along the lines explained above was defeated. A compromise was reached by the **Tithe Act of 1838**. However, this legislation did not remove the main source of tension – the Catholic peasantry's obligation to pay the tithe. The problem for the Whig government was that to change the structure of financial support for the established church was seen as the first step on the road to disestablishment.

Maynooth, 1845

The fact that the tithe question was not resolved, fuelled the campaign led by Daniel O'Connell for repeal of the **Union with Great Britain**. In 1843 the Repeal Association increased in popularity. Among its supporters were many from within the ranks of the Catholic Church. After Catholic emancipation, Sir Robert Peel, who had been Prime Minister since 1841, was convinced that the best way to pacify Ireland and solve the issue of the Church was to win Catholic opinion. Although the arrest of O'Connell in October 1843 broke the repeal movement, the tension the movement caused alerted Peel to the need to break up any growing nationalist consensus. The Devon Commission was set up in 1844 to study the issues of land occupation and landlord–tenant relations.

Peel, however, decided to go even further. In 1844 he

KEY LEGISLATION

Tithe Act of 1838 The Act included the following points:

- The tithe was to be paid in cash by the landlord on behalf of the tenant.
- Many peasants owed backpayments and all tithe debts were cancelled.

KEY TERMS

The Union with Great Britain In 1801 Ireland was formally united with Great Britain in what was to be known as the United Kingdom. The churches of the countries were united by this union.

Catholic seminary Where Catholic priests are trained.

---

proposed an increase of state funds to the **Catholic seminary** at Maynooth. The logic behind the grant was that it would win over those in the Catholic Church to supporting the Union. To Peel the future of the Union lay in appeasing respectable Catholic opinion. However, Peel was dealing with a potentially problematic issue. In 1829 he had gained many enemies within his own party over Catholic emancipation and anti-Catholic feelings generally ran high in England. Peel was resolute in his insistence that peace in Ireland was essential for domestic stability. The majority of Peel's cabinet accepted the logic of his argument although William Gladstone resigned over the issue early in 1845.

The Maynooth debate and its aftermath

Peel's Maynooth proposals were explained to the House of Commons in April 1845:

- A special grant of £30,000 was to be made to the college at Maynooth for new building.
- An annual grant of £26,000 was to be given to the college.

Although the measure passed through the House of Commons relatively easily, it had significant political consequences. Most importantly, it divided the Conservative Party. On the Third Reading of the Bill the Conservatives were split 149:148 against the Bill. Peel had to rely on opposition support to ensure the Bill's passage. Linked to the Maynooth reforms were proposals for the improvement of university education in Ireland. The Irish Colleges Act set up **non-denominational colleges** in Galway, Belfast and Cork. These universities did not develop as hoped because of the lack of financial support from the Catholic Church for non-denominational education.

THE OXFORD MOVEMENT/TRACTARIANS

A backlash against Evangelicalism and reform of the Church took the form of the Oxford Movement. Those who feared that Whig reforms would undermine the status of the Church of England included Oxford academics

KEY TERM

Non-denominational colleges Colleges where people of any religion could go to study.

John Henry Newman.

John Henry Newman, John Keble and Richard Frounde. With their supporters these academics formed what became known as the Oxford Movement. The movement issued **Tracts** which aimed to persuade religious readers of their views. Because this is how they communicated they became known as Tractarians. The main aims of the movement were to:

- seek a spiritual renewal in the Church. In the first of the *Tracts for the Times* (1833) they presented their case for the Church's eternal authority which they felt was now under threat. These Tracts were followed by many more, each concentrating on issues fundamental to Anglican belief;
- protect the position of the Church in society and an Anglo-Catholic revival which would see the restoration of traditional ritual and practices.

There were limitations to the impact of the Oxford Movement. It was more of an academic and intellectual movement than one which reached out to the new urban-based working classes. Importantly, it was accused of popery by others within the Church of England. In 1841 Newman wrote *Tract XC* in which he argued that the Thirty-nine Articles did not necessarily reject many of the practices of the Catholic Church as they were supposed to have done. The accusations against the Oxford Movement were seemingly appropriate when Newman converted to Roman Catholicism in 1845. However, the Tractarian movement continued to contribute to the Anglican revival under the leadership of Pusey. Its particular legacy was to stress the need for spirituality to be at the centre of the life and organisation of the Anglican Church.

SUMMARY QUESTIONS

1 To what extent was the Church of England reformed in the period 1820–51?

2 Why did the Anglican Church attract support and opposition in the 1820s and 1830s?

3 To what extent had the position of the Catholic Church improved in Ireland in the period 1800–50?

CHAPTER 12

What changes were there in the standard of living, 1815–51?

MEASURING THE STANDARD OF LIVING

The impact of economic change on people's living standards can be measured in two main ways.

Quantitative approach

The historian relies upon quantitative information – statistics – in particular that relating to real wages and **consumption**. If real wages rose in the period and consumption increased it is fair to argue that the standard of living increased. However, there have been considerable problems in using such data alone, one of which is that real wages varied between industries and different areas of the country. This means that one needs to use the figures below with caution.

Real wages, 1816–50 (1840 = 100) Each column shows a different calculation for real wages based on a different price index.

Year	i	ii	iii	iv
1816	101	97	92	108
1820	97			
1824	106			
1830		105	109	113
1831	109			
1840	100	100	100	100
1845	121			
1850	139	108	140	143

(Sources
i: R. Floud and D. McCloskey (eds), *The Economic History of Britain*, p.169. The figure for real wages has been reached by relating money wages to prices.
ii–iv: P. Matthias, *The First Industrial Nation*, Routledge, p. 200.)

Consumption per head per annum, 1801–50

Decade	Consumption per head (pound/p.a.)
1801–10	10.5
1811–20	11.3
1821–30	14.6
1831–40	17.9
1841–50	19.4

(Source: R. Floud and D. McCloskey (eds), *The Economic History of Britain*, p. 136.)

Similarly, most statistics on consumption per head seem to show an increase in the period in question. The historian C. Feinstein has calculated that consumption rose between 1761–70 and 1811–20 at 0.3 per cent per annum whereas from 1811–20 to 1821–50 it rose at 1.2 per cent per annum. This is borne out by the figures on the left.

These figures seem to lead the historian to the conclusion that from the end of the Napoleonic wars there was a real rise in consumption. However, there are some problems in using this data unquestioningly:

- As with the real wages data, these figures are based on the average of the population on which there is data.
- The figures hide the fact that while there was an increase in real wages and consumption among skilled workers – for example, mule spinners or iron foundry workers – others who were hit by technological advances were not so fortunate, for example, the hand loom weavers.
- For those who lived off rents, consumption most certainly did rise; but for many, rising food prices hit consumption.
- The figures also hide the problems of dating. While they show that the standard of living might have risen over a long period of time, they hide the periodic depressions such as that of 1841–3. Similarly, the figures are distorted by periodic price rises such as that of wheat in 1837–42.
- The figures do not show the significant regional variations in wages. In those counties which were home to industrial expansion, average real wages were higher for both industrial and agricultural workers; for example, wages for agricultural labourers averaged 12 shillings a week in Cheshire in 1837 but only 8 shillings in Dorset. Local studies have shown that in some areas real wages did not rise at all. R.S. Neale has argued that in Bath real wages were stagnant between the 1780s and late 1830s.

Qualitative approach

It is also possible to study contemporary attitudes to living standards to discover if they rose or fell in the period. These factors, which cannot be measured statistically, are called qualitative factors. However, commentators at the time were as divided as historians have been since between optimists (those who believed standards of living had gone up) and pessimists (those who thought they had declined).

Optimists. The contemporary optimists saw the consequences of industrialisation as a triumph of progress, technology and science. Commentators such as **Andrew Ure** described a picture of unlimited progress. This view has been backed up, be it a little more cautiously, by historians including J.H. Clapham, T.S. Ashton and R.M. Hartwell. They have argued that, in the period after the 1820s, falling prices, rising employment opportunities and economic growth led to an improvement in the living standards of the majority.

Pessimists. Against this, the pessimists of the time such as **J.S. Mill** and **Freidrich Engels** argued that industrialisation led to a decline in the quality of life of the working classes. This line has been expanded by historians such as J. and B. Hammond, E.P. Thompson and E. Hobsbawm who have argued that the consequences of urbanisation and industrialisation in the first half of the nineteenth century – for example, poor housing, adulterated food and poor education – cancelled out any material benefits. The pessimists point to the periodic outbreaks of unrest and violence, from the Swing riots of 1830 to Chartism, as evidence of the underlying dissatisfaction of the period. They point to the problems caused by technological change, including the declining fortunes of the hand loom weavers, the severity of the factory system, child labour and the widespread short-term unemployment of the period.

DID THE STANDARD OF LIVING RISE DURING THE PERIOD 1820–51?

The reliability of the evidence

The belief that there was a dramatic overall improvement in the standard of living during the period ignores the pessimism of many contemporaries. It is unlikely that there was any great rise in living standards until the mid-1840s at the earliest. However, one should treat many accounts of

KEY PEOPLE

Andrew Ure, 1778–1857 A defender of factory owners against those such as Michael Saddler and Richard Oastler who called for factory reform in the 1830s. In *Philosophy of Manufacturers*, Ure argued in favour of non-intervention by the state given the positive benefits of the factory system.

J.S. Mill, 1806–73 One of the most influential writers of the nineteenth century, his works including *Principles of Political Economy* (1848), *On Liberty* (1859) and *Utilitarianism* (1862). Mill was a utilitarian. He believed that government should intervene in social affairs only for the greater good of the population as a whole.

Freidrich Engels, 1820–95 A socialist who travelled to England to see at first hand the social consequences of industrialisation. Engels used what he saw and read to write *The Condition of the Working Classes in England* (1844), which attacked the industrial system as exploiting the working classes.

the time with caution. Writers such as Friedrich Engels in *The Condition of the Working Classes in England* attempted to describe a decline in living standards which would fit his political viewpoint. Similarly, the view held by those such as the Hammonds in *The Town Labourer* (1917) was as much the result of a moral standpoint as based on evidence from the time. Yet it is hard to dismiss contemporary reactions wholesale and the literature of those such as Charles Dickens in *Hard Times* or Elizabeth Gaskell in *Mary Barton* does reflect considerable concern that the quality of life for the labouring classes had declined.

Regional and other variations

Any study of living standards must reflect the significant geographical, occupational and chronological variations within the period. If one argues that radical industrial change was limited to a few sectors of the economy, so it makes sense that only a limited number of workers were affected by that change. As the technological innovations were mainly northern based, so it was here that wage rates became much higher than in the south. However, even this is too simplistic a picture. Studies of industrialised towns such as Preston and Oldham have shown that the improvement in the wage rates of the mule spinners should be counterbalanced by the decline in wages of the hand loom weavers. This latter group were paid on piece rate and saw their wages decline from 20 shillings a week in the 1790s to 6 shillings a week in the 1830s.

The problems of statistical data

Any data on real wages has to be treated with care. The years which historians use in comparisons can give very misleading pictures. In the 1980s Peter Lindhert and Jeffrey Williamson attempted to end the debate on real wages by showing that there was an increase of around 100 per cent in real wages between 1819 and 1851. However, these years are misleading, 1851 being one of the cheapest in the century. Had they used 1847 instead, the conclusions would have been very different. The nature of industrialisation in the period 1820–51 was cyclical and unemployment could be sudden and short lived; for example in Bolton in 1842, unemployment stood at around 60 per cent but did not last. Similarly, the calculation of real wage data only reflects the fortunes of those who received a money wage. It takes no account of the self-employed who made up approximately 40 per cent of the workforce by 1845. Nor does it take account of the unemployed or those who were only seasonally employed, an important element in the workforce.

The method of calculating consumption has varied between historians who have often used different indicators to prove their point. Similarly, they have disagreed about the relevance of various data. An example is the debate over the returns from **Smithfield market**. A rise in meat consumption between 1820 and 1851 would in theory indicate an increase in living standards.

A comparative increase in London population, beef and sheep at Smithfield, 1801–51 (1801/1801–4 =100)

Census	Animals ave. of	Index pop.	Index beef	Index sheep	Percent increase pop	Percent increase beef	Percent increase sheep
1801	1801–04	100	100	100			
1811	1810–12	119	105	119	+19	+5	+19
1821	1819–22	144	113	135	+25	+8	+16
1832	1830–4	173	127	152	+29	+14	+17
1841	1840–3	202	146	176	+30	+19	+24
1851	1850–2	246	198	193	+43	+42	+17

(Source: Neil Tonge, *Industrialisation and Society, 1700–1914*, Thomas Nelson, 1993.)

The above statistics have been used to back up the pessimists' case that consumption declined in relation to population growth. Indeed, while the consumption of beef rose dramatically in the 1840s – virtually in line with population growth – it seems that it otherwise lagged behind. However, these figures need to be put into context. The Smithfield returns ignore the consumption of pork which was a key part of working-class diet given the ease with which a pig could be kept in an urban environment. Similarly, they ignore other markets such as those at Whitechapel or Newgate: Smithfield accounted for only two-thirds of the capital's meat.

The key point to make is that consumption rose only gradually during the period. This is not surprising if we accept that the rate of growth in the economy was not as spectacular as the term 'industrial revolution' implies. It has been suggested by the historian N. Crafts that industrial output grew by 3 per cent per annum between 1801 and 1831 and by 3.3 per cent per annum between 1831 and 1860. When the following table is studied, a gradual increase in consumption can be discovered, although there seems to have been a more obvious increase from the 1840s.

UK Consumption of commodities

Year	Tea (lb)	Sugar (lb)	Tobacco (lb)
1800–9	1.42	19.12	1.11
1810–19	1.29	18.06	1.01
1820–9	1.29	17.83	0.79
1830–9	1.37	17.59	0.86
1840–9	1.55	18.45	0.91
1850–9	2.25	30.30	1.11

(Source: P Matthias, *The First Industrial Nation,* Routledge, 2nd ed. 1983.)

There are problems with using consumption as a measure of standard of living.

- First, levels of consumption can be influenced more by price changes than any improvement in living standards.
- However, in one sense consumption figures are more accurate as an indicator of living standards because they reflect the habits of a wider cross-section of the populace.

THE POLITICAL NATURE OF THE DEBATE

The standard of living debate between optimists and pessimists is essentially a political one. Most historians link standards of living to industrialisation but other factors had an effect on living standards, most noticeably the population rise and the Napoleonic wars. However, given the qualitative and quantitative evidence one should conclude that it is unlikely that there was a substantial rise in the standard of living of the labouring classes in Britain as a whole until the mid-1840s. Certain sections of the working classes did benefit from a rise in real wages although this was offset by the qualitative factors, including public heath, food and housing. As the rate of economic growth was slower than previously calculated it is unlikely that there was any overall change in living standards and this is backed up by stable consumption figures.

SUMMARY QUESTIONS

1 Did the standard of living of the working classes improve in the years 1815–51?

2 What are the difficulties for an historian in coming to a conclusion about the standard of living in the first half of the nineteenth century?

CHAPTER 13

What were the major changes in transport in the period 1815–51?

ROADS AND CANALS

Turnpike trusts Formed to arrange Acts of Parliament which would allow people to set up toll gates on certain stretches of road. The main reason for turnpiking was the increase in traffic on the roads and the shifting of the cost of upkeep of the roads from local parishes to the road users. The first Turnpike Act was in 1663 for a stretch of the Great North Road near Ware.

John McAdam, 1756–1836 Best known for the simplicity but success of his road building. He ensured that all the roads he built or repaired had both good drainage and a solid surface.

Thomas Telford, 1754–1834 Built roads with a sound foundation of larger stones and a top layer of smaller stones. His most important project was the London–Holyhead route completed in the early 1830s.

Both forms of transport were affected by the emergence of railways in the period 1820–51. But roads and canals long remained the most important modes of transport. Improvements in road transport sprang from the creation of **turnpike trusts** in the eighteenth century which invested in better road-building techniques as pioneered by **John McAdam** and **Thomas Telford**. By 1823 McAdam had repaired up to 2000 miles of road. The improvement of road foundations and better drainage meant that roads could carry heavier traffic loads. However, such improvements were not universal – only one-sixth of Britain's road had been turnpiked by 1830 – and there was no integrated road system. The significance of the improvement in road transport was not in the transportation of industrial or agricultural goods but in communication and personal travel.

Developments in road travel

The reduction in times of travel by the mid-1830s stimulated a boom in the **coaching industry**. In the mid-1750s, travelling from London, it had taken two days to reach Oxford, four and a half days to reach Manchester and ten to twelve days to reach Edinburgh. By the mid-1830s these times had been cut to six hours, nineteen hours and forty-five hours respectively. The result was the creation of a coaching industry which responded to the increased demand for travel. In 1740 there had been one coach a week from London to Birmingham, by 1829 there were 34 a day. Coaching was controlled by large firms which became considerable enterprises. The growth of personal travel was not matched by an increase in goods carriage. By 1823 there were 735 public carriers in

A turnpike at Clifton Down, Bristol.

London. There were large companies such as Pickfords but they were the exception rather than the rule.

Decline in the road industry

It was long-distance travel rather than local road traffic that was hit by the growth of the railways. By 1851 only 6700 miles of railway had been open which left much business for road coach companies. Many road hauliers adapted to the railways; for example in 1840 Chaplin and Horne became agents for the Grand Junction Railway. Similarly, Pickfords managed to adapt by working in conjunction with the London and Western Railway from 1847. That said, the effects on the roads of direct competition could be devastating. By the end of 1830, two-thirds of the coaches running from Liverpool to Manchester had been withdrawn as a result of the opening of the railways. In 1841 the Bath mail coaches were withdrawn with the opening of the Great Western Railway. Similarly, during the period 1837–51 the revenues of the turnpike trusts fell by one-third. In some areas opposition to the turnpikes manifested itself with attacks on the toll gates. The most famous of these outbreaks was the **Rebecca Riots** of between 1839 and 1844. These attacks declined after the Turnpike Act of 1844 which encouraged the control of all turnpikes within a shire by one authority which could harmonise tolls.

KEY TERM

Coaching industry The largest companies in London were owned by W.J. Chaplin, E. Sherman and B.W. Horne who together provided around four-fifths of the main coach services. By 1838 Chaplin's coach services employed 2000 people and 1800 horses.

KEY EVENT

Rebecca Riots A memorable feature of the Rebecca Riots was that the male rioters often dressed up as women so as to avoid being identified.

Canals

The canals had benefited from sustained investment over a considerable period of time. By 1830 there were some 4000 miles of navigable waterways in Britain. However, the canal system was by no means uniform. Individual canals had been built in response to local business demands; for example, the Trent and Mersey, completed in 1777, had been partly financed by **Josiah Wedgwood**. Therefore little attention was paid to building an integrated system. Although the canals were slow, they carried a significant proportion of Britain's industrial goods, perhaps as much as 35 million tons a year by the early 1840s. Indeed, this trade continued for some time despite the introduction of the railways which were slow to challenge for the carrying of goods. In the 1840s canals were used to transport goods needed for the building of the railways; for example, the Kennet and Avon carried its greatest tonnage in the 1840s. However, the limitations of the canals were too great a handicap in the competition with the railways. Most damaging was the slow nature of the canals: it could take 36 hours to send cotton from Liverpool to Manchester. Despite measures such as a Parliamentary Act of 1845 allowing canal companies to act as carriers, the reliability and speed of the railways meant that the competition was unequal.

THE AGE OF THE RAILWAYS

The railways were the result of innovation in iron for rails and steam engines for traction purposes. However, the triumph of steam over horsepower was not immediate or automatic.

- **Stockton to Darlington 1825.** Horse drawn wagons had been used for some time in the coal industry and the debate about the most reliable and effective form of traction was not settled for some time after the opening of the Stockton to Darlington Railway in 1825. The significance of this line, for which George Stephenson was the engineer, was its use of a steam engine *Locomotion* from the start.

- **Liverpool to Manchester 1830.** The potential for successful investment and the inadequacy of the canals stimulated the planning of further lines, most importantly that linking Liverpool and Manchester. The new line had to overcome considerable opposition from the canal companies in Parliament as well as engineering problems. The line's engineers, George and Robert Stephenson, managed to tackle the problem of Chat Moss, a twelve-mile bog, by laying heather and timber foundations and the solid rock of Olive Mount by blasting through half a million cubic yards. In 1829 a competition held at Rainhill to decide on the form of locomotion for the line was won by Stephenson's multi-tubular boilered *Rocket*. The line was opened in 1830 and was immediately successful as a passenger- and freight-carrying operation. Until 1845 passenger receipts on the line were double those of freight; indeed, in the first year of opening it carried 400,000 passengers.

Opening of the Liverpool–Manchester railway The opening of the railway line on 15 September 1830 was marred by a fatal accident involving William Huskisson MP, who was hit by the *Rocket*.

In the 1830s and 1840s the main trunk lines of the English railway system were built. Important lines were completed linking London to the provinces, including the line to Birmingham in 1838 and Bristol in 1840. Investment cycles had a time-lag factor of some three to four years.

Railway mileage, selective years 1833–50

Date	Companies created	Mileage sanctioned	Mileage opened	Total opened (cumulative)
1833	4	218	42	208
1836	29	955	65	405
1839	2	54	227	970
1840	0	0	528	1497
1844	50	805	192	2236
1845	120	2896	294	2530
1846	272	4540	606	3136
1848	82	373	1253	5129
1850	3	7	618	6559

(Source: P Matthias *The First Industrial Nation,* Routledge, 2nd ed. 1983.)

Railway mania, 1844–7

Railways were built by private companies which needed Acts of Parliament to give them the power to compulsorily purchase land. Once this permission was given, the speculation began as the companies offered good dividends. In the 1830s they paid dividends of 9 per cent but because of some less than economic schemes in the 1840s the average dividend fell to 3.31 per cent in 1850. In the 1840s there was a trend towards the amalgamation of companies as a way of maximising profits; for example, in 1847 the Lancashire and Yorkshire Company was formed from six smaller companies. The dominant figure in this process of amalgamation was **George Hudson**. The '**railway mania**' of the 1844–7 period was the result of government fiscal policy and a series of good harvests. Despite the expense of railway construction – on average a railway cost £40,000 a mile – the rail-building industry took on spectacular proportions. Huge armies of construction workers – contractor Morton Peto employed some 14,000 navvies – undertook monumental engineering feats. This was driven by speculation which resulted in 650 Railway Acts being passed in the period 1845–8.

Government intervention

By the 1840s a national railway system was emerging. In response, the government introduced measures to regulate the industry, mainly out of fear of the growth of monopolies in the industry.

- In 1840 the Railway Regulation Act insisted that companies intending to build a new line had to inform the Board of Trade which would then inspect the line. Companies also had to report their toll rates and accidents.
- An Act in 1842 extended the power of the Board of Trade to the extent that it could delay the opening of any new line it was not satisfied with.
- In 1844 the **'Cheap Trains' Act** insisted that railway companies provide at least one train a day with cheap third-class travel.

However, the problems of railway regulation are best seen in the passage of the last law. Suggestions that the railways might be drawn into state ownership met with fierce resistance from the railway lobby in the House of Commons. This lobby was not without considerable influence, given that in 1847 178 MPs were railway company directors. Yet the logic of a nationally organised network was clear given the inconsistencies of the canal network.

There was also a difference of opinion over the size of the track gauge, the so-called '**Battle of the Gauges**'. The standard size used by the Stephensons was 4 ft 8½ ins but the Great Western Railway completed by I.K. Brunel had a broader gauge of 7 ft. In 1846 the Gauge Act regulated that the standard width for all railway lines was to be the narrower gauge. In the same year a new department, the Commissioners of Railways, was set up to control rates charged by the railway companies.

THE EXPANSION OF THE RAILWAY NETWORK

The railways were a sector that continued to flourish up to the eve of the First World War. New lines continued to be opened and the railways continued to attract new investment. In 1870 there were 15,500 miles of railway operating in Britain; by 1912 this figure had risen to 23,400 miles. Some of the new lines that opened were not so profitable as earlier constructions; an example being the Great Central from Sheffield to London which opened in 1899. However, of the capital spent on the railways in 1870–90, only 5 per cent went into companies that were unprofitable.

Problems for the railways

As with other industries, the railways had to adjust to changing circumstances in the second half of the century. The result of this is that there is a perception of a relative decline in the success of the industry. The evidence to back up this claim is shown most clearly in the railways' **operating ratio**.

KEY THEME

'Battle of the Gauges' It should be pointed out that different companies built to different size gauges.

Railways' operating ratio, 1870–1912

Year	Operating ratio
1870	51
1880	52
1890	56
1900	57
1905	62
1910	63
1912	62

(Source: Railway returns, quoted in T.R. Gourvish, *Railways and the British Economy, 1830–1914*, Macmillan, 1989)

KEY TERM

Operating ratio A calculation economists use to assess the performance of the railways. It compares the working costs (for example, wages and improvements) as a percentage of revenue. So, if the operating revenue is given as 60 for any one year, it means that working costs of the railways were 60 per cent of the revenue.

KEY TERM

Working costs The costs incurred by a company in running the railway. This includes wages, repairs and fuel.

The figures show that there were problems for those who operated the railways and that, during this period, the railways were becoming less profitable to manage. There are many reasons for this, the most important being the rise in labour costs, especially in the 1870s. This drove up the **working costs** for the railways but the problem was hidden in the 1870s by the fact that the price for other goods such as coal actually fell. Although the railway companies attempted to become more efficient, they suffered from the rising cost in the operation of the railways. This was particularly the case in the period 1896–1901.

A further problem for the railway companies was government legislation which put a cap on rates the companies could charge passenger and freight customers.

- The most significant law was the 1894 Railway and Canal Act which fixed passenger rates at 1892 levels.
- The Cheap Trains Act of 1883 ensured a proportion of daily trains charged low fares and the Railway Regulation Act of 1893 limited the hours those employed by the railway companies could be made to work.

So, higher costs and regulation increased the operating ratio of the railway companies. This did not mean, however, that the railways performed worse than in earlier decades. Instead, the period after 1851, and after 1870 in particular, saw the railways operate in a different economic and political environment.

THE IMPACT OF THE RAILWAYS ON THE ECONOMY

The railways had an important impact on the development of the British economy. However, it is difficult to measure this impact and one should not exaggerate it.

Industry

Construction. The building of the railways had a significant impact on the economy and financial structures in Britain. Railway construction in the 1840s was a major industry in

UK railway traffic 1842, 46, 50

Year	Revenue (£m) (from passengers and freight)
1842	4.8
1846	7.6
1850	13.2

(Source: Railway Returns)

itself. During the period 1845–9 average annual employment on the railways was 172,000; in May 1847 this stood at a peak of 256,509. Such employment gave a significant boost to the economy, the average yearly wage bill in the same period was £11m or 2 per cent of GDP.

The iron industry. Railway construction stimulated demand in iron: from 1844 to 1851, 18 per cent of pig iron produced was taken by the railways, this figure peaking at 30 per cent in 1848. Areas such as south Wales received a significant boost to their local economies as a result of such demand. However, the impact of the railways should not be exaggerated. Railways were not the cause of any technical change in the iron industry. The historian G. Hawke has shown that it was the export demand for iron, which was in part related to foreign railways, that produced the significant boost in demand for British iron. But one should not underestimate the importance of the railways on the demand for iron, especially within this period. This was especially the case with the south Wales iron industry which was technologically advanced, produced on a large scale and had lower fuel costs. It provided iron for railways being built in the south of England, the Great Western Railway and even parts of the London–Birmingham railway.

The coal industry. Similarly, demand for coal was significant; between 1844 and 1851 railways took up some 6–10 per cent of output. But this should be placed within the context of a significant growth in demand for coal from other industrial sectors.

The engineering sector. The impact of the construction of the railways on the engineering sector was great. The demand for engines and rolling stock meant that it consumed as much as 20 per cent of output during the period 1844–51.

Brick production. This saw a rise in output to build viaducts, stations, bridges and so on. As a result 25–30 per cent of output was used in railway construction during the 1840s.

Economic development

The railways were directly responsible for stimulating permanent and structural economic growth. Construction of the railways occurred during specific periods, for example, 1844–9, which were often followed by quieter periods of development. It is evident that the impact of the railways was to help move Britain into a more mature stage of economic development.

- As a result of railway development, there was significant improvement in the cost and, in particular, the quality of the transportation of goods in Britain.
- From the early 1840s to the late 1850s passenger fares on the railways fell by 30–40 per cent and the introduction of the railways led to a reduction in freight charges; for example, the Aberdeen–London coastal shipping business saw a cut in rates of up to 60 per cent in response to the new competition.
- Canal companies were forced to cut rates as the railways undercut their prices by as much as 1.33 pence per ton per mile. These reductions in costs were bound to have a positive effect on whole sectors of the economy.
- Agriculture benefited greatly from a reduction in the price of fertiliser, feed and farming implements. The more efficient transportation of fresh produce was to have an impact on diet and availability of food in the cities. Market gardening flourished; for example, farmers in Bedfordshire could not only send their produce to London but north to the new industrial towns.

Financial markets

The railways were an important stimulus to change in the financial markets and in how they operated. This is not surprising given the extent of capital investment during the 1840s.

- The London stock market expanded and shifted its operations from mainly government bonds to company securities. The demand for capital saw the opening of provincial stock exchanges; for example, Liverpool and Manchester in 1836, Glasgow in 1844 and Leeds and Birmingham in 1845.

- The prospect of a good return on investment encouraged thousands to invest in railway papers (a type of share) thereby very much widening the social base of shareholding. So it is probably valid to argue that the railways had a considerable impact on the capital market. This does not automatically lead to the conclusion that the growth of the railways was essential to Britain's economic growth.

The problem for the historian is in the measurement of the railway's impact. The most important attempt to measure the significance of the railways in the economy was undertaken by G.R. Hawke. Using the **social saving** theory, Hawke calculated that the railways had by 1865 led to a social saving of between 7 and 11 per cent. However, such figures were calculated on what has been seen to be dubious data; for example, Hawke used secondary sources and figures from parliamentary committees which are perhaps unreliable. This does not lead to a conclusion that the railways did not have a significant impact. It does, however, lead to the conclusion that the impact over a period of time is difficult to quantify.

The cities

What is without doubt is that the railways had a significant impact on the perceptions of contemporaries, as can be seen in the writings of authors such as Charles Dickens in *Dombey and Son*. This impact was probably due to the physical transformation caused by the construction of the railways. Not only were many towns transformed, but some emerged from virtually nothing, for example, **Swindon** and **Crewe**. Some of the major cities were virtually redesigned in the wake of the railway companies' demand to build passenger stations and lines; in London around 800 acres were commandeered for the railway; in all, some 76,000 people were displaced. Although the railways opened up new areas for industrial expansion – for example, the iron and later steel industry at Middlesborough – their impact on the industrial geography of Britain was limited. The railway helped to link the industrial centres already created.

KEY TERM

Social saving The difference between the cost of transporting goods by one means of transport (in this case the railways) and another type of transport, imagining that the railways did not exist. It has been used by historians as a way of measuring the impact of the railways.

KEY PLACES

Swindon Developed as a result of the Great Westen Railway choosing the town for its engineering depot.

Crewe Crewe did not exist before 1840. By 1901 it had developed into a town with a population of just under 50,000. The town grew as a result of the Grand Junction Railway setting up a carriage works factory there.

Swindon in the 1840s.

Leisure

The railways opened up the possibility for travel. In 1851 the Great Exhibition attracted crowds from around the country, many of the visitors coming to London by train. Excursions offered by the railway companies created opportunities for cheap holidays. Blackpool and Southport on the west coast grew rapidly in response to demand for holidays by the inhabitants of the towns and cities of the industrialised north. By 1871 Blackpool received 500,000 visitors a year. Other towns such as Eastbourne and Windermere did not exist before the railways had made their development economically viable.

THE IMPACT ON THE ECONOMY, 1851–1914

The railways expanded to the point that, by 1870, the basic network and organisational structure had been established. Indeed, the railways were the means by which the economy was able to move to a mature stage. They provided a means of transport which was both cheaper and more efficient than its rivals.

- In 1850 the railways were carrying an estimated 38 million tons of freight per year; by 1875 that figure had risen to 199.6 million tons.
- The number of passengers using the railways showed a similarly remarkable increase. In 1850 72.9 million

people travelled on the railways; by 1875 the number of passengers had risen to 507 million people a year.

- However, such a growth, while being impressive, was not revolutionary. The years 1851–1914 did not see particularly heavy investment in the railways or any significant change in technology.
- What did take place was an increase in the use of a system that was relatively underused in 1850. The growth of the railways was to have a substantial impact on certain sectors of the economy although it is difficult to quantify this impact. While the railways' contribution is without doubt, they did not fundamentally alter the pattern of Britain's economic structure.

THE SOCIAL IMPACT OF THE RAILWAYS

The impact of the railways on society was considerable but often gradual. The railway created a national market and broke down barriers to migration. It also improved communication with the faster and wider distribution of newspapers, a quick postal service and the introduction of the telegraph. Through this more effective spread of information, the opportunities offered by urban life became more widely known, and the journeys to town easily available. The period between 1841 and 1911 saw a migration of some 2.8 million people from southern rural areas. Many of these went to London, and many of them were women going into domestic service. However, railway travel was generally used by those travelling long distances.

Commuting. The age of mass commuter travel by train was delayed until the end of the century. In the 1850s only around 27,000 people would arrive daily in London by train whereas around 244,000 would arrive in the capital on foot or by horse drawn carriage. Pricing policies also meant that the working classes would only travel at certain times on the cheap trains stipulated by the 1844 Railway Act. The Great Northern Railway's cheap tickets (at a quarter price) only applied to those planning to arrive in London before 6 a.m. In this sense the railways reinforced class divisions rather than altered them in any way.

Suburban lines. The suburbs which developed around great cities were dominated by either the working or middle classes depending on the pricing policies of the railway companies. An example was the fact that the Great Eastern Company's lines to Edmonton and Chingford to the north of London provided a return fare to the capital of 2d for workmen. However the Great Northern line which linked the capital to suburbs such as Wood Green and Southgate did not. The result was that different social groups migrated to these areas, the working class predominantly to the former and the middle class to the latter.

Leisure. The railways did lead to the growth in leisure trips, especially to the coastal resorts, but the real impact did not occur until the end of the century. This was because it took some time for many resort areas to be linked by railways to major towns and cites. An example is the seaside town of Bournemouth, which had a population of around 6000 in 1871. However, the building of a railway line into the town in 1870 meant that the population had risen to 78,674 by 1911. From the 1840s excursions and holidays were organised to seaside resorts which reflected the different classes in society; thus Blackpool was popular with the working classes, and Scarborough with the better-off middle classes. In 1841 Thomas Cook organised his first excursion, from Leicester to Loughborough, using the Midland Railway Company. Two decades later trips were being organised overseas. However, holidays for the working classes were restricted by the amount of time given for holidays by employers.

SUMMARY QUESTIONS

1 Explain how the attitude of the government to the railways changed during the nineteenth century.

2 To what extent did the construction and operation of the railways transform Britain's economy?

CHAPTER 14

Why did the Conservative Party win the 1841 general election?

THE WHIGS IN GOVERNMENT AFTER 1832

By 1836 the Whigs had lost their appetite for reform and begun to drift aimlessly. This is hardly surprising:

- they did not come to power with any reform programme;
- most ministers opposed radical initiatives;
- the crisis caused by parliamentary reform had been exhausting and alarming.

In any case, for most Whigs it was the natural order of politics merely to enjoy the fruits of office. A tired Grey was succeeded as Prime Minister by **Lord Melbourne** in 1834. However, the King feared further attacks on the Anglican Church and he sacked the Whigs at the end of 1834, appointing Peel as Prime Minister of a minority government. The Whigs found that their image of 'friends of the people' had been seriously undermined after they returned to office. The transportation of six agricultural labourers – the celebrated **Tolpuddle martyrs** – from Dorset to Australia for attempting to form a trade union, and popular hatred of the new workhouses began to destroy the hopes of a more enlightened approach to government raised in 1830. More serious politically, the Whigs also alarmed both the landed and commercial classes by their electoral pact with the Irish and radicals in 1835, their threat to the Anglican Church and their financial incompetence which culminated in a budget deficit of £7m by 1841.

KEY PEOPLE

Tolpuddle martyrs In January 1834 a new trade union, the Grand National Consolidated Trade Union (GNCTU) was formed. It was inspired by Robert Owen's idea of collective action as being at the heart of working-class improvement. In March 1834 six labourers from Dorchester were sentenced to seven years' transportation to Australia for swearing secret oaths in setting up a group which was part of the GNCTU. Public opinion was shocked and secured their return in 1836.

Lord Melbourne Melbourne was chosen to succeed Grey because he was uninspiring and a safe pair of hands. Melbourne considered the position a 'damned bore' but he was the only alternative to Lord John Russell who was feared by William IV and conservative Whigs as a dangerous reformer. He did not have good relations with the King but was much liked by the new young Queen Victoria who came to the throne in 1837.

THE TORY PARTY IN OPPOSITION

The Tories had opposed the reform of Parliament in 1832. For those such as Robert Peel, reform meant a significant challenge to the constitutional order. Peel opposed reform on principle. However, he hoped that he could help build a party which believed in a new form of conservatism and had a broader appeal. The Tory Party was already a broad church, from those such as Richard Oastler on one wing to those labelled Ultras on the other. What Peel attempted to do was adopt principles that would appeal to all strands of the party and the wider population beyond. In opposition, Sir Robert Peel cleverly exploited Whig weaknesses.

He accepted the reform of Parliament as a fact of life but committed himself and his party to protect the institutions of the country, such as the Crown, established church and the Union. In Parliament, Peel adopted the tactic of constructive opposition against Grey's government. Instead of voting against every measure, he decided his best tactic was to judge each issue against his principles and vote accordingly. In the 1833 Parliament Peel only voted three times against the government. This put distance between himself and the Ultra Tories who wanted to see the end of Whig government at any price. However, Peel believed that, for the Tories to regain office, they had to be seen in a more positive light than the Ultras' tactics showed.

The Tamworth Manifesto

In November 1834 King William IV sacked the Prime Minister Lord Melbourne and asked the Duke of Wellington to form a ministry. Wellington was reluctant to do so and recommended that the King choose Peel. It was Peel's intention from the start to convince the country and electorate that there was a difference between his brand of conservatism and that of his predecessor the Duke of Wellington. With this aim in mind, Peel issued his Tamworth Manifesto in December 1835. The document was published by the press and read around the country.

The main aim of the manifesto was to appeal to the electorate in the new Parliament:

- Peel accepted that the Reform Act was 'a final and irrevocable settlement of a great constitutional question'.
- He promised that the Conservatives would undertake a 'careful review of institutions, civil and ecclesiastical'.
- Where there was a case for change, he promised 'the correction of proved abuses and the redress of real grievances'.
- Peel offered to look at the question of church reform in order to preserve the 'true interests of the Established religion'.
- Peel's basic message, therefore, was that the Conservatives would reform to preserve.

Election of 1835

The election of 1835 saw considerable gains for the Conservatives. The party won over two-thirds of the seats it had contested although it only stood in three-fifths of the country's seats. However they failed to gain an overall majority. The Conservatives won all 29 county seats and were the largest single party in Parliament with 290 seats. This success might be partly attributed to the reorganisation of the **Conservative** Party undertaken by **F.R. Bonham**. Peel's hopes of attracting support from disaffected Whigs were dashed when the Whigs made a post-election agreement, known as the Lichfield House Pact, with Irish and radical MPs. Peel's government fell over its proposals for Irish church reform and the Whigs, under Melbourne's leadership, formed a new ministry. The **Hundred-Day Ministry** increased Peel's standing both in the House of Commons and in the country as a whole. His authority within the party was also strengthened with even leading Ultras accepting his leadership.

Opposition, 1835–41

In opposition, Peel continued to improve the Conservative Party's organisation and refine its policy. Peel strengthened his control of the party by appointing able chief whips such as Sir George Clark (1835) and Sir Thomas Freemantle (1837). In 1835 Bonham persuaded Peel to set up a permanent committee chaired by Granville Somerset. Its aim was to co-ordinate the party's electoral affairs. The result of such work could be seen in the general election following William IV's death in 1837. The Conservatives

KEY TERM

Conservative was the label given to the party fighting the election under the terms of the Tamworth Manifesto.

KEY PERSON

F.R. Bonham The highly successful agent of the Tory Party. Outside Parliament, F.R. Bonham skilfully reorganised the party's electoral machine. Based at the Carlton Club, Bonham was crucial to Peel's success.

KEY THEME

Peel's 'Hundred-Day Ministry' The significance of this ministry was that it demonstrated Peel's ability as a statesman. It also revealed his willingness to consider moderate reform.

gained thirteen seats and reduced the Whigs' majority to just over 30. Peel's political skills meant that moderate Whigs such as Sir James Graham and Stanley and their supporters could be drawn into political alliance. During the period 1835–40, nearly 60 Whigs 'crossed the floor' (changed sides in the House of Commons). Peel recognised that his era was one in which party politics would dominate. He met frequently with Bonham and the whips at his home in Staffordshire and there worked out his clear political strategy.

Whig weakness

After the 1837 election the Whigs led by Lord Melbourne were increasingly dependent on the support of Irish MPs. This worked to the advantage of the Conservative Party which presented itself as the party of Protestantism. After 1837 the group of MPs led by Lord Stanley crossed the floor of the House of Commons. It meant that Peel's front bench was now a strong debating team with Stanley, Gladstone and Graham undermining the credibility of Melbourne's government. In 1839 Melbourne's government was defeated by five votes over the **Jamaican crisis** when it planned to suspend the Jamaican Assembly. The government resigned and Queen Victoria reluctantly asked Peel to form the next ministry.

The Bedchamber crisis, 1839, and its aftermath

Peel accepted the Queen's invitation but only on the condition that she sack those in her immediate circle of courtiers who were related to or associated with Whig politicians. The Queen refused and asked Melbourne to form his third ministry in May 1839. With hindsight one can judge the Conservatives lucky not to have been brought into government in such circumstances and what became known as the Bedchamber crisis was a blessing in disguise. The worsening economic crisis led to serious social unrest; for example, the Newport rising and the emergence of Chartism. Increasingly, government found it difficult to balance the budget; in 1841 the annual budget deficit had risen to £7m. The Whig ministries had grown in unpopularity through reforms such as the Poor Law Amendment Act of 1834. Peel had actually supported some of these reforms, including the Municipal

Corporations Act of 1835. However, it was the government that received the blame from opponents.

ELECTION OF 1841

The strength of Conservative Party organisation and Peel's leadership are important in explaining why the Conservative Party won the general election in 1841. However, the Whigs made important tactical mistakes in 1841. The Select Committee on Import Duties that reported in 1840 argued that tariffs on certain goods should be reduced in order to stimulate consumption and, ultimately, revenue. In the budget of 1841 the Whigs reduced duties on corn, sugar and timber. The attack against such a policy by Peel resulted in a defeat for the government in the House of Commons and the calling of another general election. The issue of the Bedchamber was resolved by the intervention of Queen Victoria's new husband Prince Albert. At the election, Peel's party projected an image of moderation, responsible government, statesmanship and policies of protection of the Established Church and social order. The **Conservative Party triumphed** with a majority of 76.

SUMMARY QUESTIONS

1 What were the main points and significance of the Tamworth Manifesto?

2 Why did the Conservatives win the 1841 election?

CHAPTER 15

What were the main features of Peel's ministry, 1841–6?

PEEL'S AIMS

The focus of Conservative reform after 1841 was to

- restore economic prosperity;
- ease social unrest.

The second Chartist petition (presented in 1842) and the widespread distress caused by a recession prompted Peel to act. His guiding philosophy in economic affairs was that of the classical economists, such as David Ricardo and Nassau Senior. Their belief was that government could help a return to prosperity by reducing tariffs and thereby stimulating trade. Although protection of agriculture had been an important element in the support of the Conservative Party in 1841, Peel could also argue that reduction in duties had been a policy of the Tories in the 1820s.

ECONOMIC PROSPERITY

Budgets, 1842–5

In his 1842 budget Peel stunned the country by re-introducing an income tax previously only imposed during times of war. All those with incomes of more than £150 a year were to be taxed at the rate of 7d in the pound. Peel hoped that the tax would bring in a revenue of around £3–4m a year which would be used to pay off the budget deficit. The 1828 **sliding scale of duties** on corn was modified and duties were reduced on goods ranging from coffee to meat. Although there was some opposition from rural Conservative MPs the measures were accepted without too many problems. By 1845 Peel's government had removed the budget deficit and had created a surplus of £5m. However, Peel argued in the budget of that year

Sir Robert Peel.

for an extension of income tax for another three years. This was partly to fund the reduction of duties on items such as sugar. In the 1845 budget Peel also abolished all duties on raw materials such as cotton.

Bank Charter Act of 1844

Throughout the first half of the century, the banking world had been troubled by instability. In 1825, 73 banks suspended payments and around 50 collapsed altogether. This brought on the spread of **joint stock banking**. This made banking safer in that joint stock banks had more partners and were therefore more able to accumulate capital. Despite banking reform in 1833 there were further banking crises in 1836 and 1839. In 1836 the stock market crashed leaving debts unpaid. In 1839 the poor harvest meant that gold was needed to pay for imports of foreign capital. The drain on reserves was considerable. There were two schools of thought as to what reform was needed – the **banking school** and the **currency school**. Peel sided with the latter.

The main features of the Bank Charter Act of 1844 were:

- The Bank of England was given the monopoly over note issue and no new privileges of note issue were to be granted. Those banks that issued notes (by 1844 still around 25 per cent of notes were issued by banks other than the Bank of England) were encouraged to stop issuing notes. Once they had done so they could not re-issue.
- The Bank was limited to issuing a certain sum in notes; in 1844 the figure was fixed at £14m. Any further issues of notes were to be backed by gold bullion.
- Accounts were to be published weekly.
- The Bank of England was divided into two main departments: one dealing with banking, the other with the issue of notes.

The importance of the Bank Charter Act

Peel believed that the Bank Charter legislation was of central importance. In attacking 'reckless speculation' and by assuring a stable currency, Peel built the foundations for what he believed would be a more stable economy. To Peel

KEY THEMES

Joint stock banking was when owners of banks took on business partners. These partners would invest in the companies and share the profits (as well as the liability).

The banking school believed that the size of the note issue should be left to the bankers to decide, given their understanding of the economy.

The currency school believed that the size of note issue should be directly related to the amount of gold in the country. If too many notes were issued, there would be periodic crises of the type seen in 1836 and 1839. The currency school argued that the government should restrict note issue to the Bank of England. It also suggested that the government decide on the size of the note issue.

the most important aspect of the Act was that confidence in the currency could be ensured by making paper currency easily transferable into gold. Although the Act had to be suspended at times for being too rigid, it did form the basis of financial stability until after the First World War. Peel also reformed Company Law. Bankruptcy courts were established and the Companies Act of 1844 led to greater state control of private companies.

SOCIAL REFORM

Against the background of the social unrest of the so-called 'hungry forties', Peel was determined to address some of the social problems of urban workers. Peel hoped that free trade would reduce the cost of basic goods for the lower classes. In addition the employment of women and young boys in mines was outlawed (Mine Act, 1842) and their working hours were restricted to ten in factories (Factory Act, 1844). The working classes also benefited from the Railway Act of 1844 which limited the cost of travel of some trains to a penny per mile, and by the low-cost provision of local wash houses by the Baths and Wash House Act, 1846.

PEEL'S STYLE OF LEADERSHIP

Despite his leadership skills and the evident success of his economic policy after 1841, Peel was never able to fully exert his authority over his own party. There are various reasons for this:

- **Personality.** Peel had a haughty and aloof personality, partly as a reaction to aristocratic prejudice against his middle-class Lancastrian background. Peel never felt easy in the company of landed gentry and even denounced the bigotry, idleness and ignorance of some of his own county backbenchers.
- **Autocratic style.** Rather than cultivate support Peel was autocratic in style, appointing like-minded ministers and demanding absolute loyalty.

KEY TERM

Hungry forties is a contentious term. It is used to explain the widespread distress in many areas – especially in the early years of the decade.

KEY LAW

Baths and Wash House Act, 1846. This allowed for the building of bath and wash houses to be funded out of the local rates. Clients were not to be charged more than 1d.

- **Ideology.** Although 'Conservative' in name, many of Peel's MPs were of decidedly old 'Tory' ideas – staunch supporters of the Anglican Church and the privileges of landed wealth. Some Conservatives had never forgiven Peel for his great betrayal of Catholic emancipation in 1829 and suspected that he might be capable of a similar treachery over the Corn Laws. Protection of wheat was regarded by landowners as vital to safeguard both their income and their political dominance in the social hierarchy. It is important to remember that the Great Reform Act in some ways strengthened the landed interest by increasing the number of county seats and by enfranchising tenant farmers. It is, moreover, clear that the Conservative victory, in which the party won 136 out of 159 English county seats, was a triumph not so much of Peelite reform but of hard-line landed defence of the Corn Laws.

REPEAL OF THE CORN LAWS

Opposition to the Corn Laws was based on the increasingly acceptable idea that the prosperity of the nation would be better secured by free trade. The ideas were clearly set out in General T. Perronet Thompson's *Catechism on the Corn Laws* (1827). In many of the newly industrialising towns, campaigns were launched in opposition to what was seen as unfair protection of the landowners. The sliding scale of duties introduced by William Huskisson in 1828 did little to end opposition. In Nottingham in 1833 an Anti-Corn Law Association was set up. It was in years of economic depression that the campaign was further stimulated.

The arguments of the free traders which attracted support were as follows:

- The Corn Laws forced up wages because of the high cost of food. This fact would make British industry less competitive.
- The end of restrictions on corn would encourage other countries to lower their tariffs on British goods.

- The Corn Laws prevented Europeans exporting corn to Britain therefore earning less British currency to spend on British manufactured goods.
- By dissuading foreign agriculturists, the Corn Laws were a factor in persuading them to turn to manufacturing and therefore compete with British industry.

The Anti-Corn Law League

The arguments against the Corn Laws were forcibly put by the Anti-Corn Law League, yet the opposition to the Corn Laws existed from their introduction in 1815. In the 1826 general election, opponents of the Corn Laws had made it an issue in the campaign.

In 1836 an Anti-Corn Law Association was formed in London and other associations were formed in Manchester in 1838. As part of the agitation, radical MP Charles Villiers introduced an anti-Corn Law motion in Parliament in 1839. The motion received 195 votes but was heavily defeated. The result was the foundation of a national organisation in Manchester – the Anti-Corn Law League – to campaign for the repeal of the Corn Laws on a national basis. Its leading members included **John Bright**, **Richard Cobden** and businessmen Thomas Potter and James Wilson.

Character of the League and tactics

The Anti-Corn Law League was an unmistakably middle-class movement. Although it did attract working-class support – for example, the Operative Corn Law Association founded in 1839 – there was considerable tension and friction between the League and other campaigning organisations, particularly the Chartists.

The tactics of the League were designed to raise the profile of the cause of repeal:

- **Single issue.** Despite being a radical movement supported by many leading radical politicians, the League campaigned on a single issue; that of repeal of the Corn Laws. This helped win it support as its aims were clear.
- **Registration.** The League worked hard to register voters and remove Conservatives from the electoral register. It

KEY PEOPLE

John Bright, 1811–89
Brought up as a Quaker, Bright became a leading Liberal politician. He was a very effective public speaker and was an important asset to the Anti-Corn Law League. Bright was inspired by the ideas of individual liberty and the cause of parliamentary reform.

Richard Cobden, 1804–65
Cobden was founder of the Anti-Corn Law League in 1839 and was elected MP for Stockport in 1841. After the Repeal of the Corn Laws in 1846 he remained committed to the cause of free trade. In 1860, as a private individual, he negotiated the Cobden–Chevalier Treaty which improved trade between Britain and France.

attempted to fight by-elections and general elections on a repeal ticket and did so with mixed success. In the 1841 election the League won seats including Walsall and Stockport. However, such a tactic was expensive and not always productive. Despite the 1832 Reform Act, a number of seats remained in the control of patrons. The League attempted to counter this influence by buying properties for supporters of such value as would enable them to receive a vote. By 1845 it was calculated that the League had spent around a quarter of a million pounds on such an exercise. There were gains at the 1845 election as a result. Such electoral manipulation was crucial in the League's development as an influential political force.

- **Legality.** Although there were times when some League members argued in favour of illegal practices, their views did not become policy. In 1842 there was agitation from within the ranks of the movement for a tax strike. However, the League's leadership constantly stressed the importance of legality.
- **Organisation.** The organisation of the movement was effectively run by Joseph Hicken and J.B. Smith. It was run by a council and a number of committees. The national organisation was divided into twelve districts, each run by a league agent. The League raised considerable funds for its campaign; in 1844 it had £100,000 at its disposal. The League organised numerous fund-raising activities and sold memorabilia on a grand scale.
- **Propaganda.** The League was highly effective at spreading its message. The *Anti-Corn Law Circular* preached the message of repeal as did *The Economist*, founded in 1843. In the same year the League ran a highly effective campaign in London which won the support of sections of the London press. Meetings were held throughout the country and in 1843 Free Trade Hall was built in Manchester for the specific purpose of hosting anti-Corn Law rallies.

Peel's position

While Peel had to face the effective campaigning of the Anti-Corn Law League he also had to deal with the opposition of disaffected landed gentlemen. There were

Tory revolts against the reduction of cattle duties in 1842, Canadian corn in 1843 and sugar in 1844. Peel also faced a major revolt from the same hostile group of Ultra Tories when 150 backbenchers voted against the Maynooth grant in 1845. In the wake of this revolt, Peel's Home Secretary, Graham, remarked that the party was 'shivered and angry'. Peel realised that the repeal of the Corn Laws, to which he became reconciled soon after coming to power, risked the unity of the Conservative Party and his own political career. Peel believed that agriculture no longer needed protection and that free trade would boost manufacturing output and lower prices, so helping to demonstrate to the working classes that aristocratic government was sensitive to the needs of the ordinary people. His 1842 and 1845 budgets showed that he accepted the argument of free traders that to reduce tariffs was in the country's interest. In this he was in complete agreement with Richard Cobden, the energetic leader of the Anti-Corn Law League.

The Irish famine

Famine was not new to Ireland. It had struck many times in the nineteenth century, for example in 1807 and 1830–4. However, the famines had always been restricted to certain areas of Ireland. In September 1845 it was reported from the west of Ireland that the potato crop had failed. The cause of the failure of the crop was a **potato blight**. Land settlement and the Penal Laws in Ireland in the eighteenth century had resulted in the settlement of large numbers of peasants on tiny plots of land. In Connaught in the west of Ireland in 1841, 64 per cent of farms were smaller than 5 acres. The potato was the staple diet for around one-third of the population. Widespread potato blight was therefore a disaster. Peel had hoped to educate his party to the necessity of repeal, but the potato famine in Ireland brought the question to a head in 1845.

Peel responded promptly to the plight of the Irish. He has been blamed on occasions for not reacting promptly enough, but he did take a number of measures:

- In November 1845 he set up a scientific commission to investigate the causes of the blight.

A peasant family in Ireland surveying the meagre crop of potatoes they have to live on following the failure of the potato harvest.

- In 1846 Peel authorised the setting up of public works on harbours and roads. Through this he hoped to provide employment and therefore wages for those in distress.
- He encourgaed the setting up of voluntary committees to deal with the effects of famine. By 1846 around 650 such committees had been set up.
- He imported into Ireland £100,000 of Indian corn which was released onto the market as a means of preventing prices rising too high.

Unfortunately these measures were inadequate in coping with the scale of the famine, and failed to stop absentee landlords exporting food.

Peel moves to repeal

The Irish famine gave Peel the excuse to propose the removal of the Corn Laws whose continuing existence was due to political rather than economic reasons. In November 1845, when the cabinet first met to discuss repeal, Peel failed to get the support he needed for abolition. Peel's position was made harder by a change in the position of the Whig leader Lord John Russell. In his *Edinburgh Letter* of 25 November 1845, Russell announced his conversion to the cause of repeal. When in December Peel proposed a gradual phasing out of the protective tariffs the majority of the cabinet supported

KEY THEME

Russell and Peel Russell's decision to support repeal forced Peel's hand. He now would rely on Whig support and they demanded repeal in one go.

him. However two important ministers, Stanley and Buccleuch, threatened to resign from the cabinet rather than accept such a move. As a result Peel offered to resign, but was forced to continue as Prime Minister when Russell failed to form a ministry. By the end of the year only Stanley within the cabinet remained in opposition to Peel's proposals.

The opposition of the protectionists

Even though he had won over the support of his cabinet, Peel still had to convince the Conservative Party in Parliament. Opposition to Peel was rallied by **Lord George Bentinck** in the House of Lords and, more fatally, in the Commons by the articulate and ambitious **Benjamin Disraeli**. The debates on the Corn Laws in February 1846 showed the intensity of opposition to repeal.

The protectionist arguments included the following points:

- The Conservatives had stood in the 1841 election on a platform of protection and maintenance of the Corn Laws. To change their position would be a betrayal of rural interests.
- Peel's argument that agriculture no longer needed protection was scorned by those who pointed to the success of the Corn Laws in keeping agricultural prices high. Peel's proposals for farmers to adopt the techniques of high farming were not realistic given the large sums of investment capital that were needed.
- Many argued that the situation in Ireland was not as bad as Peel had made out and that he was using the idea of a famine to push repeal through.

In the first vote on the Bill to repeal the Corn Laws on 28 February 1846, 112 Conservatives voted in favour but 231 voted against. The proposal had split the party.

The Corn Laws are repealed

The opposition of Irish MPs to a Bill to deal with disturbances in Ireland led to a delay in the return of the Corn Bill to Parliament. Disraeli had made mischief since failing to win cabinet office in 1841. Now, as the Corn Bill was debated again, he mercilessly exploited Peel's personal

Benjamin Disraeli.

deficiencies and record as a traitor. He denounced Peel for betraying the landed interest and abandoning party principles. In the debate on 15 May Peel again reminded the House of Commons of his reasons for proposing repeal. The repeal Bill received a majority of 98 votes although only 112 Conservative MPs voted in favour. In the House of Lords, the Whig leader Lord John Russell helped the passage of the Bill by refusing to allow his party to amend it. The Corn Act received the royal assent in June 1846. At the same time Peel's position as Prime Minister had become untenable after a defeat by a majority of 73 in the House of Commons over the Irish Coercion Bill. Despite the fact that 116 protectionists voted with the government, quite possibly in response to the over-aggressive attacks on Peel by Disraeli and Bentinck, the party was truly split. It might be argued that Peel failed to provide **justification for repeal** to his party. In reforming to preserve the interests of the landed classes, Peel showed complete confidence in his own judgement.

CONSERVATIVE DIVISION

The most important political consequence of repeal was that it split the Conservative Party. Nearly all of the leading members of the government including Sir James Graham and William Gladstone remained as Peelites. However, the protectionist wing of the party remained as the majority.

The result of the party's split was that it failed to win a general election until 1874. While not setting up a new party, the Peelites stood against Conservative Party candidates at this time. While Peel was alive he showed great bitterness towards his opponents within the party. Many Peelites eventually joined with the Whigs to form the Liberal Party who ruled outright for 28 of the years between 1846 and 1874. Gladstone, the most outstanding Peelite, became Chancellor in 1853 and followed a programme of free-trade policies.

Peel's justification for repeal On 15 May Peel justified repeal in social terms saying: 'The real question at issue is the improvement of the social and moral condition of the masses of the population.'

SUMMARY QUESTIONS

1 Why did Peel repeal the Corn Laws in 1846?

2 Why did the Conservative Party split over Corn Law repeal?

AS ASSESSMENT

Sources exercise in the style of Edexcel (Unit 1 – Poverty and the State, 1800–50)

Source A

PUNCH'S PENCILLINGS.·· N° LXII.

THE "MILK" OF POOR-LAW "KINDNESS."

'The "milk" of Poor Law "kindness"', a cartoon from 'Punch', 1843. The drawing shows a mother in the workhouse being separated from her baby.

Source B

The effect of the new law was almost magical. The ratepayers now had substantial proofs in their own pockets of its advantage. The labourers began to think it was high time 'to look out'. Employment was now sought after and the farmers honourably answered the demand. The gratitude of the workman was shown by his civility, his attention and his industry.

Adapted from an article on *The Principles and Progress of the Poor Law Amendment Act* (1837) by Edwin Chadwick.

Source C

An Assistant-Commissioner Mr. Weale found that the number of poor under the new law, in 1836, amounted to 4,254,000 or a burden on each of the population of nearly 7s 7d. Where, then, was this boasted economy under the new arrangement? It evaporated immediately the test was applied. Let them go to Manchester, where the cost, taking into calculation the population of the poor, was 6s. 6d., thus showing a difference of 1s 6d in favour of the old system.

Adapted from a speech by J.H. Cutler, December 1840.

Source D

The new Poor Law was firmly based on the idea that since paupers were criminals it followed that the workhouses must be prisons . . . Workhouse paupers were regarded as objects of horror and disgust. A few examples may be given. In the summer of 1843 a five-year old boy, who was an inmate of the Greenwich Union workhouse was punished by being locked up in the mortuary for three nights and he had to sleep on some coffin lids.

Adapted from *The Condition of the Working Class in England* by Friedrich Engels (1844).

Questions

1 Study Source A. What can you learn from this source about criticisms of the new Poor Law? (3)

How to answer this question. The question is asking you to show that you understand the source. Therefore you must:

- provide some explanation which answers the question
- refer to the source to back up what you are saying.

Style. Here is an example of the style you should use:

The categorisation of different groups in the workhouse provoked fierce opposition to the new Poor Law. The evidence of this source, Punch, which was a magazine widely read by the middle class, shows that such opposition was not just from the poor.

2 Use your own knowledge to explain the provisions of the new Poor Law which dealt with the able-bodied poor. (4)

How to answer this question. The question is asking you to focus on the able-bodied poor. It relies on your having a good understanding of the new Poor Law of 1834. You need to organise your information clearly before you start.

> 3 Assess the value of Sources C and D as evidence about the impact of the 1834 new Poor Law. (5)

How to answer this question. When answering a question about the value of a source you should try to avoid generalisations about the type of source and you should concentrate on more than just its content. Instead you should ask yourself at least some of the following questions:

- What is the nature of the source?
- Who is the author of the source?
- What is his/her purpose in producing the source?
- Is the source produced as propaganda?
- Has the author deliberately distorted the evidence?
- What is the situation of the author?
- Is the author in a position to know about the subject of the source?
- Has the author dealt with the different views from the time?
- How has the author dealt with gaps in his/her evidence, has he/she simply ignored them?
- How much is the interpretation an example of the kind of attitudes held at the time of writing?

Style. Try to refer to the sources when possible to back up your ideas. To gain top marks you need to ensure that you cover both sources. Below is an example of the style you might choose to use. The candidate is addressing the issue of the purpose of the author.

> *The value of both sources is that they reveal some of the arguments against the new legislation. One source of bitterness was that the new law did not reduce costs and that it was inappropriate for dealing with poverty in industrialised areas. This is shown in Mr Cutler's attack on the Poor Law in which he points out that the new law costs more –'where, then, was this boasted economy?'. However, the author uses select information in attacking the new law, concentrating on Manchester, which was a special case.*

> 4 How far does the evidence of Source B support the claims of Mr Cutler in Source C? (6)

How to answer this question. This question demands that you cross-reference between the sources. Therefore you should try and do the following:

- Show that the sources are concerned with the same issue – the cost of the new Poor Law.
- Explain the extent of, and the reasons for, the differences between them.
- Refer to the sources wherever possible.

> 5 Use your own knowledge and the information from Sources A and D. How far do you agree with the view stated by Engels in Source D that 'Workhouse paupers were regarded as objects of horror and disgust'? (12)

How to answer this question. You are asked to give an analytical answer to this question. The main focus of your answer must be on the treatment of the workhouse poor. To be awarded the top marks you need to do the following:

- Argue using the sources and your own knowledge.
- Show that you can sustain a judgement throughout the question.
- Show that you understand that the treatment of paupers varied from workhouse to workhouse.
- Show that you understand the context of Engels' claims and his purpose in making them.

Style. Below is an extract of a good answer to this question. The candidate has sustained an argument in a direct style throughout the answer.

Engels is accurate when he implies that paupers were treated in a dehumanised fashion. The idea of less eligibility was to place them in a position beyond that which was considered acceptable in society. Therefore the new law went about attempting to categorise and separate those in the workhouse. It was this deliberate attack on the emotions of those who had been pauperised which was so despised. Such anger and condemnation can be seen in Source A whereby, at a certain age, the child is removed from her mother and taken to another section of the workhouse as ordered by the new law's provisions.

Source exercise in the style of AQA

Study the sources below and then answer the questions.

Source A
Thousands of children are daily compelled to labour from six o'clock in the morning to seven in the evening with only thirty minutes allowed for eating and recreation. Poor infants! Ye are compelled to work as long as the necessity of your needy parents may require, or the cold-blooded greed of your worse-than-barbarian masters may demand! Ye are doomed to labour from morning to night

for those who care not how soon your weak and tender frames are stretched to breaking.

Adapted from a letter by Richard Oastler, MP
to the Leeds Mercury published in 1830.

Source B

That abuses have existed in some factories is certain; but these have been rare instances; and, speaking generally, factory workpeople, including non-adults, are as healthy and contented as any class of the community obliged to earn their bread by the sweat of their brow.

A political economist J. R. McCulloch attacks
Sadler's Factory Report, Edinburgh Review 1835.

Source C

I well remember being set to work in my father's mill when I was little more than ten years old . . . Many [other] workers died before they attained the age of 50 years, having the appearance of being much older, a premature appearance of age which I believe was the result of the nature of the employment in which they had been brought up.

From The Curse of the Factory System by John Fielden,
a Yorkshire mill owner, 1836.

Source D

Never will I believe that what makes a population stronger, and healthier, and wiser, and better, can ultimately make it poorer. You try to frighten us by telling us that in some German factories the young work seventeen hours in the twenty-four and you ask whether, if we pass this bill, we can hold our own against competition such as this.

From a speech by Lord Macaulay on the Ten-Hours Bill, 22 May 1846.

Questions

Reading. Before answering these questions you should have read Chapter 6 (pages 46–54) of this book.

1 a Study Source A. Explain the meaning of 'barbarian masters' in the context of factory reform. Use your own knowledge to answer this question.   (3)

How to answer the question. There are likely to be only a few marks for this question so do not spend too much time on it in an examination. To reach full marks you should do the following:

- You might comment on the ruthless manner in which many factory owners ran their factories.
- The question also asks you to show an understanding of 'the context' of factory reform. In your answer, therefore, you should explain how criticism of the actions of the factory owners was at the heart of the campaign for reform.
- A further point might be to explain the term 'barbarian' in the context of the motives of many factory reformers.

> **b** Study Source B. Explain how useful this source is to an historian trying to gain an understanding of conditions in factories in the 1830s. (7)

How to answer this question. Before answering this question and other questions about utility you should go through the following checklist of points:

- Top quality answers will discuss both the positive value and the limitations of the source.
- Evaluate the source's reliability by looking at the purpose and the situation of the author.
- Compare the usefulness of the source against your own knowledge.
- Are the author's views typical of the period?
- What gaps are there in the evidence?

Here is an extract from a good standard answer to this question.

McCulloch's views are most useful in that they represent the attitude of an important group from within the political world, the political economists. People such as McCulloch and Nassau Senior provided the arguments against factory reform. The source is a clear example of Utilitarianism, the belief in the greatest happiness of the majority 'speaking generally . . . factory workpeople are as healthy and contented as any class…obliged to earn their bread'.

> **c** Study all the sources. You should use your own knowledge in answering this question. 'The ideas and influence of the political economists were the major reasons why factory reformers faced so much opposition in the 1830s and 1840s'. Explain whether you agree or disagree with this view. (15)

How to answer this question. This question wants you to make links between the sources and your own knowledge to explain what happened.

Plan. Before you start an answer to this question it is important that you write a plan. Your plan should include the main points of argument or analysis that you are going to use to answer the question. Examples of your main points in answering this question are:

- To a great extent the ideas and influence of the political economists were important because they provided the framework for the argument against state intervention.
- This argument was most clearly put by the factory owners.
- However, other factors were of importance: the fear of foreign competition, hostility to centralisation and opposition from parents fearing a reduction in family income.

Structure. These three points give you plenty to explain. To reach the highest level you need to do the following:

- Introduction. In your introduction you should briefly explain your main points. There is no need to go into detail here.
- Argument. You should try and explain the extent to which the ideas and influence of the political economists were important.
- At some stage in your essay you will include a 'however' paragraph that argues the relative importance of the other factors listed above.
- Conclusion. Your conclusion should be brief and sum up your line of argument.

Information to use. The question has asked you to use your own knowledge and the sources. The following information can be used from the sources:

- Source A shows the needs of some parents and the greed of factory owners. These were important groups opposing change.
- Source B shows an opinion typical of those held by political economists and which influenced factory owners and politicians alike.
- Source C shows that some factory owners such as John Fielden supported the idea of some reform.
- Source D is arguing in favour of reform by attacking the argument used by opponents that reform would make way for increased competition from abroad.

You can use your own knowledge from reading chapter 6 of the book. These are the main themes:

- The political economists had an important effect on the argument against reform. Of particular importance was the equation of the number of hours with profitability and the view that profitability was assured in the last hour of the day.
- *Laissez-faire* attitudes were also important.

- The limitations of the 1833 and 1844 Factory Acts and the difficulties of their enforcement.
- The differing attitudes of factory owners.

Style. Here is an example of a direct style using evidence.

The opposition to factory reform came primarily from mill owners who argued that a reduction in working hours would reduce their profitability. Their arguments were framed in the context of those of the political economists such as Nassau Senior and David Ricardo. They argued that cutting the working hours of children would lead to the reduction in the wages of those who were most needy. Their cause was led by mill owners such as William Ackroyd of Otley and James Ackroyd of Halifax and championed by the editor of the Leeds Mercury, *Edward Baines and other Whig newspapers including the* Manchester Guardian. *In Parliament the opposition to factory reform was well represented in the Parliament elected in 1832, by men such as the MP for Leeds, John Marshall, and the MP for Halifax, John Wood. They were supported by many in the new Whig cabinet who believed in* laissez-faire *and were bolstered by the campaign of the 'Association of Master Manufacturers'.*

Essay questions in the style of Edexcel (Unit 2 – the age of the railway, 1830–70)
Reading. Before answering this question you should read Chapter 13 (pages 109–121) in this book.

> **1 a** Describe the economic and social impact of the construction of the railways in the years 1830–51. (15)

How to answer this question. The question is asking you to describe the impact of railway construction within specific years. Even though there is plenty to write beyond the year 1851 you must try to restrict your answer to material within the dates set by the question.

Plan. Before you start writing your answer you must plan it clearly. In your plan you need to identify the main areas of the impact of railway construction that you are choosing to describe. If you organise your work well, you stand a much better chance of reaching the highest level. You need to be comprehensive in your use of evidence, thereby covering the following areas:

- An explanation of the impact of railway construction on various industries including coal, iron and brickmaking.
- A description of the impact of railway construction on employment and on the wider economy.

- The answer should highlight the social impact of the railways but also stress that this impact was, to an extent, limited up to 1851. However, the railways did have an effect on urbanisation and communication, and had begun to have an effect on personal travel.

When writing there are a few points that you should follow:

- You must make sure that your answer is direct to the question.
- There is no need to describe other events of the time; stick to the main features of the government and the constitution.
- You must make sure that your answer contains factual detail.
- Write in short paragraphs. Don't forget to include a very brief introduction and conclusion.

Style. Below is an example of how you might write a section on the main features of the constitution.

The construction of the railway did have an impact on the demand for iron, especially within this period. This was particularly the case with the south Wales iron industry which was technologically advanced, produced iron on a large scale and had lower fuel costs. Therefore it provided for railways being built in the south of England, the Great Western railway and even parts of the London-Birmingham railway. Similarly, demand for coal was significant, between 1844 and 1851 it took up some 6–10 per cent of output, but this should be placed within the context of a significant growth in demand for coal from other industrial sectors. The impact of the construction of the railways on the engineering sector was great. The demand for engines and rolling stock meant that it consumed as much as 20 per cent of output between 1844 and 1851. Similarly the brick industry saw a demand for its product to build viaducts, stations, bridges and so on. As a result some 25–30 per cent of output was used in railway construction in the 1840s.

b Explain why the railway network expanded so rapidly in the period 1830–70.   (15)

Reading. Before answering this question you should read the pages 111–120 of this book.

How to answer this question. The question is asking you to explain the causes of railway expansion in the period 1830–70. You need to focus on the causes of rapid expansion and create an argument that you sustain throughout the question. You need to use well-selected and accurate information.

Plan. Because this is a question that asks you to analyse, you need to identify your main arguments. You also need to decide what you think are the most important factors to explain instability in this period. These are examples of what might be the main points of your plan:

- The railway network expanded so rapidly because of a combination of factors which included high levels of investment, the role of certain individuals, the expansion of the capital market, and the levels of technological advance.
- However, expansion was not constant and there were periods of building mania followed by periods of relative inactivity.

Style. These points need to be explained in clear paragraphs that follow a brief introduction. Below is an example of the style you might choose to use to answer a question such as this one.

> . . . However, the speed in the growth of the network should be challenged. In 1850, the railways were carrying an estimated 38 million tons of freight per year, by 1875 that figure had risen to 199.6 million tons. The number of passengers using the railways showed a similarly remarkable increase: in 1850, 72.9 million people travelled on the railways, by 1875 the number of passengers had risen to 507 million people a year. However, such a growth, while being impressive, was not revolutionary. The years 1850–70 did not see particularly heavy investment in the railways or any significant change in technology. What did take place was an increase in the use of system that was relatively under-used in 1850.

Exercise in the style of Edexcel (Unit 3) Using a source as a stimulus

Reading. Before you answer this question you should read Chapter 5 (pages 37–45) and Section 1 (pages 155–165) of this book.

Study Source A and then answer questions which follow.

Source A

17 February. Anything which amounts to the formation of a new Constitution I shall oppose.

3 March. The general belief is that the Bill must be thrown out on the second reading. I expect Ministers will then resign and anarchy begin. I feel inclined as a choice of evils to support and even speak in favour of the Bill.

5 March. The measure excites the country very much.

8 March. I consider the Bill dangerously violent, but apprehend less danger from passing it than rejecting it.

Adapted from the diary of the Whig MP for Stafford, 1831.

1 a Study Source A. What is the author's attitude towards the reform of
Parliament? (3)

How to answer this question. The question wants you to focus your answer on
Source A.

In asking you to explain your answer the question is also hoping that you will explain
the author's attitude towards reform, i.e. that he changed his attitude to the idea that
reform was necessary in order to avoid anarchy.

You should quote from the source whenever possible. However, you should ensure
that your quotes are short and to the point.

Style. You need to answer the question directly. Here is an example of a sentence
showing how you might do that.

The author's attitude to reform changes in the light of events outside Parliament. As
with many other Members of Parliament, he accepted the need for reform but only in
order to preserve the old system: 'a choice of evils to support and even speak in favour
of the Bill'.

b What were the main arguments used by those who opposed parliamentary
reform in the years 1830–32? (5)

How to answer this question. Although there is a source at the start of the exercise,
the question does not ask you to use it if you do not want to. In this case there is
little in the source to help you and you are expected to use your own knowledge

The question here wants you to describe the main arguments against reform. It
would be a good idea for you to organise your description thematically. Themes you
might include are:

• Opposition on grounds of principle, fear of further reform, reform was too
revolutionary.

c What was the effect of the Reform Act on the British political system? (7)

How to answer this question. For this question you are to use the source but only as a
stimulus. The question asks for an analytical answer. Therefore you need to do the
following:

- Answer with a strong line of argument and make a clear judgement that comes down on one side or the other of the question.
- Show that you understand that the Act did have an impact but that the extent of that impact was limited.
- Use well selected evidence to back up your argument.

Style. Below is an extract from an answer to this question.

A significant effect of reform was that it acted to polarise the political system by clearly defining party divisions. The fierce debate stirred by the reform crisis after 1830 broke the post-war consensus and accelerated the emergence of two more clearly defined political ideologies. Attitudes and voting on the Reform Act reflected very precisely party political affiliations. The enlarged electorate after 1832 further encouraged party political debate during election campaigns, while the need to register voters resuscitated the establishment of more elaborate national party organisations. Peel's direct appeal to the electorate and his defining of a party political programme in his Tamworth Manifesto in 1835 is sometimes seen as marking the rise of modern party politics.

Structured question in the style of OCR (Unit 2 – the age of Peel)

1 Identify and explain any two factors which led to the repeal of the Corn Laws.
(30)

How to answer this question. You will be judged on your ability to show your knowledge and understanding of any two reasons for the repeal of the Corn Laws. You can do that by doing the following:

- You need to explain key issues convincingly and relevantly. You might chose from a list of factors that might include the following:
- The Irish famine, the role of the Anti-Corn Law League, Peel's acceptance of free trade, the role of Lord John Russell and the Whigs, high farming.
- Prioritise your factors and ensure that you plan your answer first.

2 How successful was Peel as leader of the Conservative Party? (30)

How to answer this question. You will need to plan your answer and work out a line of argument before you start. Quickly note the content you will include in your answer. In this case it is expected that you will concentrate on the Great Ministry of 1841–46 but you should also mention the Conservatives in opposition as well as the Hundred Days ministry.

Plan. There is much to cover in your answer. Therefore you need to structure your answer in such a way that you will be able to include the content suggested below. Here is a suggested plan.

- Introduction.
- Paragraphs 1 and 2. Highlight the successes of Peel as Conservative leader before 1841.
- Paragraphs 3 and 4. Argue the achievements of Peel as Prime Minister.
- Paragraph 5. The question-marks over Peel's leadership, especially over the division of the party.

Content. Here is a list of the content you might include in your answer:

The Tamworth Manifesto, creation of a Conservative consensus, Conservative Party in opposition up to 1841, the election victory of 1841, Peel's budgets 1841 and 1843, free trade and protectionism, social reform, repeal of the Corn Laws and division of the Conservative Party.

Structured Question in the style of AQA (Unit 2 – Britain 1815–41).
Before you answer this question you should read Chapter 4 (pages 23–36) and Section 2 (pages 166–170) of this book.

> 1 Read the following statement and then answer the questions that follow.
>
> At the Congresses of Troppau and Laibach in 1820–21, differences emerged between Castlereagh and those representing the countries of the Holy Alliance. The most significant cause of tension was the policy of intervention in the internal affairs of other states.
>
> **a** Use this source and your own knowledge to explain Castlereagh's foreign policy priorities in the period 1820–1822. (5)

How to answer this question. Although there are not many marks for this question and you should not therefore spend too much time on it, you must ensure that you quote from both the source and your own knowledge when answering the question.

Style. Here is a substantial extract from an answer to this question. Note how the candidate has referred to the source and his/her own knowledge.

Castlereagh's main foreign policy priority was to preserve the established order in Europe. Although he disapproved of the European autocratic regimes, they were preferable to a revival of revolution and war. Such a threat of revolution was real in Europe as could be seen by the revolutions in Spain and Naples in 1820. However, as the source shows, it should be remembered that Castlereagh also objected to the leading powers interfering unnecessarily in other countries' affairs. He did prevent Russian intervention in Spain and Portugal in 1820 and he opposed Austrian intentions in Naples. What is more, Castlereagh withdrew from the Congress System when he believed that it was being used to organise joint intervention in other states. As a result he refused to sign the Troppau Protocol in 1820.

> **b** Why did Castlereagh have problems in his dealings with other members of the Quadruple Alliance in the years 1815–22? (7)

How to answer this question. To be awarded top marks for your answer to this question you need to do the following:

- Show that you have a clear understanding of, and can prioritise, a range of factors.
- You must make links between the factors and come to a conclusion in your answer.

> **c** How did Canning's foreign policy priorities differ from those of Castlereagh? (15)

How to answer this question. The question is asking you to make a comparison between the two. To reach a top level mark you need to do the following:

- Ensure that you refer to both Canning and Castlereagh with a balance between the two. Plan lines of argument to use throughout your answer. Here are some examples:
- There were noticeable differences between the two with regard to attitude to the Quadruple Alliance, rebellions in Spain, Greece and elsewhere and towards the Congresses.
- However, the most important point to make is that in practice they agreed on the first priority of the protection of British interests.

Course essay question in the style of AQA

Before you answer this question you should read Chapter 8 (pages 79–90) and Section 6 (pages 192–199) of this book.

> 1 Why was the new Poor Law introduced in 1834?

How to answer this question. To achieve high marks you need to note the following:

- The key to a successful course essay is a long and detailed plan.
- Your main points of argument need to be clearly thought through.
- You need to link the main factors together in your plan and throughout your essay.

General points on structure. It is important that you think about how you will structure your answer before you try to tackle the question. You will be able to plan before you write your timed essay. To answer these types of essay questions you need to make sure you:

- read the question carefully and identify what the question is asking you
- write a response to the question that is direct and to the point
- plan your answer carefully before you start to write.

In your plan you should include a list of points which will form the basis of your argument/judgement. You should then briefly map out what you are going to put in each paragraph.

- Start your answer with a brief introduction.
- Keep your paragraphs to the point.
- Choose evidence to back up the points you have made and use it in your answers.
- Conclude in such a way that you clearly state the judgement you have made in response to the question.

Plan. You need to plan your essay to avoid simply running through a narrative account of the 1830s. You need, in particular, to identify the points of argument which would allow you to do this. Here are some examples:

- The causes of the new Poor Law were fundamentally ideological. It was the perception of the existing system through the eyes of political economy which brought criticism of the old Poor Law and proposals for such a radical restructuring.
- The rising cost of poor rates in times of depression post 1815 radically transformed attitudes towards the Poor Law and paved the way for the abolition of outdoor relief.

Content. You must ensure that the content you use covers the 1830s. You should make reference to the following in your essay:

The workings of the Speenhamland system, the impact on the poor rate of economic depression post 1815, demobilisation and the Swing riots, Benthamism and the ideas of Senior and Chadwick, the diversity of the old Poor Law.

Further course essay questions will be asked on religion and politics in England and Ireland c. 1820-c.1841. To answer these questions you should read Chapter 11, pages 91–101 of this book. Here are some examples of the types of questions asked on this subject:

2 Why did the Church of England provoke strong opposition in the 1820s and 30s?

3 How effectively were the grievances of non-conformists and Roman Catholics addressed in the period 1828–41?

A2 SECTION: BRITAIN IN THE AGE OF REFORM, 1815–51

INTRODUCTION

There has been considerable debate about the extent to which Britain experienced economic, social and political change between 1815 and 1851. The following sections attempt to concentrate on the main areas of debate which have been included in the specifications of the Awarding Bodies.

Section 1: To what extent was this period an 'Age of Reform'? This section attempts to evaluate the extent to which Britain experienced political reform in this period.

Section 2: British foreign policy 1815–27 attempts to weigh up the successes and failures of the foreign policy of Castlereagh and Canning.

Section 3: How Liberal was Liberal Toryism? Discussed here is the extent to which the era of Liberal Toryism marked a new departure.

Section 4: Peel and the Conservative Party 1832–46 examines Peel's contribution to British politics, his significance as leader of the Conservative Party and the reasons for the repeal of the Corn Laws.

Section 5: The Chartist experience attempts to discuss the main areas of debate about the nature of the Chartist movement and the reasons for its failure.

Section 6: Economic change looks at the main features of industrial, agricultural and demographic change in the period.

SECTION 1

To what extent was this period an 'Age of Reform'?

KEY THEMES

- The period between 1815 and 1851 has been described as an 'age of reform' reflecting the amount of measures introduced by successive governments.
- Governments did attempt to modernise existing institutions in order to respond to long-term economic and social changes.
- Important reforms were introduced to the parliamentary system and the Church of England.
- Governments also began to take a more active role in economic and social questions, such as trade policy, working conditions, education and poverty relief.
- The immediate impact of political reform was usually not great, but it did pave the way for more radical reforms throughout the rest of the nineteenth century.

WHY WAS THERE SO MUCH REFORM, 1815–51?

1 Reaction to social and economic change

Reform was needed after 1815 because governments had failed to respond to rapid economic and social changes. Governments of the eighteenth century did little more than collect taxes and defend the realm. There was no concept of intervening to redress abuses, solve grievances or improve the condition of life of the population. Moreover, the upheaval, terror and war which followed the French Revolution convinced a generation of political leaders that any reform was dangerous and that the existing system should be preserved at all costs. By the time war had ended society had undergone important changes. A long-term rise in population, migration to towns and sustained mechanisation of crafts led to urban overcrowding. At the same time economic power was beginning to shift away from the landed elite to the professional and manufacturing classes. Many Whigs became convinced that the institutions of the country could be strengthened if political influence were extended to the respectable and propertied middle classes.

2 Response to agitation

Reform was stimulated by popular agitation. By the 1820s Tories such as Peel recognised that crude repression of agitation was in itself inadequate.

The reforms of the so-called Liberal Tories after 1822 were in part an attempt to address some of the grievances upon which post-war unrest was founded. More dramatically it was the fear of revolution in Ireland posed by Daniel O'Connell's Catholic Association that helped to convince Wellington and Peel of the need for Catholic emancipation in 1829. Similarly, the violence following the rejection of the Reform Bill by the House of Lords in October 1831 helped to show some waverers that there could be no turning back. Lord Melbourne conceded that the scale of the disorder had frightened him to death and Lord MacCauley advised the Lords to reform that 'you may preserve'. The Chartist agitation of the 1840s was for Peel an important consideration in his economic and social legislation, and indeed in the repeal of the Corn Laws in 1846 Peel attempted to reconcile workers to the virtues of an aristocratic government.

3 Influence of new ideas

The success of the state in mobilising for such a prolonged war with France suggested ways in which the government could intervene in peacetime. Whilst the idea of non-intervention by the state – *laissez-faire* – remained dominant, some reformers were attracted by the advantages of central bureaucratic regulation. The most influential group were the followers of the radical Jeremy Bentham, for example Edwin Chadwick and Nassau Senior. These people attacked the ill-informed and out-of-date style of eighteenth-century government and campaigned effectively that legislation should be useful and rational, founded upon detailed research, and enforced by efficient, accountable, central control. The influence of this group provided the impetus for and ideas behind the new Poor Law system in 1834 and the reform of municipal corporations in 1835.

4 Moral reformers

Some reforms can be credited to the campaigns of individual crusades by evangelical Christians. William Wilberforce was the outstanding supporter of the abolition of slavery, while Richard Oastler and Lord Shaftesbury did much to restrict the use of child labour in factories and mines, by alerting the public to the barbarities of their employment. Oastler campaigned energetically through newspapers in Yorkshire, while Shaftesbury produced a damning report into the use of child and female labour in mines.

5 Party politics

Governments were also responsive to the electoral advantage of reform. After 40 years in opposition some Whigs saw the party advantage in widening the electorate to the middle classes in 1832. Likewise the new Poor Law and the reform of municipal corporations were inspired in part by the Whig need to placate the new voters. Peel was quick to accept the Great Reform Act and embrace a new, more reformist 'conservative' approach. His Tamworth Manifesto of 1835 appealed directly to the interests of commercial and professional groups. These promises were delivered by his free trade policy after 1841 and most decisively by the abolition of the Corn Laws in 1846.

THE GREAT REFORM ACT

Chronology of reform crisis, 1830–2

1830	June	Death of George IV; accession of William IV.
	July	Dissolution of parliament.
	September	Huskisson killed at inauguration of Liverpool and Manchester Railway.
	November	Wellington declares against parliamentary reform; government defeated on a vote on the Civil List Accounts; Wellington resigns.
1831	March	First Reform Bill introduced into the House of Commons by Lord John Russell.
	April	Government defeated on Gascoyne's amendment opposing the reduction in numbers of MPs for England and Wales. Parliament dissolved.
	June	Whigs returned to government after general election; second Reform Bill introduced.
	July	Reform Bill receives second reading.
	September	Reform Bill receives third reading.
	October	Reform Bill rejected by House of Lords. Riots in Nottingham, Derby and Bristol.
	December	New Reform Bill introduced into Commons; passes second reading.
1832	January	William IV agrees to creation of peers in order to obtain passage of Reform Bill.
	March	Reform Bill passes third reading by 355 votes to 239.
	April	Reform Bill passes second reading in Lords.
	May	Government defeated on Lydhurst's motion; resignation of Ministers. '**May Days**'; Wellington asked to form an administration but unable to do so; the King forced to recall Grey and confirm assurances that peers will be created as necessary to ensure passage of Reform Bill.
	June	Reform Bill receives third reading in Lords and royal assent.
	July	Scottish Reform Act passed.
	August	Irish Reform Act passed.

KEY TERM

'May Days' A period of political crisis caused by the threat of Wellington's return as Prime Minister. Francis Place proposed a 'run on the banks' in opposition to Wellington.

DID BRITAIN COME CLOSE TO REVOLUTION IN THE YEARS 1815–32?

Groups with the potential for revolution

The scale and the violence of popular agitation after 1815 certainly alarmed contemporary politicians and members of the upper classes. Many had in the back of their minds the events of the French Revolution of 1789. Certainly the agitation against the Corn Laws in 1815, against the introduction of threshing machines in 1830 and in favour of parliamentary reform after 1830 generated fierce passion. Some campaigns were well organised and attracted impressive support. Daniel O'Connell's Catholic Association had huge influence over the Catholic population of Ireland. The National Association of United Trades for the Protection of Labour organised by John Doherty had a membership of 80,000 by November 1830. Equally important was the Birmingham Political Union organised by Thomas Attwood which could mobilise over 100,000 at a public meeting in May 1832. These were impressive movements in an age when nationwide communications and transport were slow and expensive.

Violent unrest

Popular agitation was also capable of leading to violence and death. The East Anglian riots of 1816, the infamous Peterloo Massacre of 1819 and, most seriously, the rioting in Bristol, Nottingham and Derby at the height of the reform crisis in 1831 clearly illustrated that agitation threatened property and life. During the reform crisis the Duke of Wellington constructed iron grills to protect his house while Peel barricaded his house, Drayton Manor, in Staffordshire against attack. In Parliament, Lord Macaulay warned peers 'The danger is great. The time is short. Reform that you may preserve'. There was no doubt that a few extremists had a revolutionary agenda. A mob seized guns during the Spa Fields riot of 1816. There was an attempt to seize Nottingham Castle in 1817 and in 1820 Arthur Thistlewood hatched a plot to assassinate the entire cabinet in the 'Cato Street conspiracy'. These examples show that some unrest did aim at more than the redress of specific grievances and envisaged some revolutionary change in the existing social and political order.

The most serious of all the popular agitation, the campaign for parliamentary reform, 1830–32 reached a crescendo when the ruling classes had become seriously divided. Reformers were able to exploit a bitter clash between the Whigs and Tories on a constitutional issue. Indeed the political establishment temporarily lost the vital weapon of solidarity against its critics.

Limitations of revolutionary violence

Despite sustained and, at times, violent outbursts of popular unrest, contemporaries overestimated the danger of revolution during this period. Haunted by memories of the French Revolution and alarmed at the unreliable reports of spies and ill-informed magistrates, contemporaries often detected revolutionary threat when in fact there was none. Most of the popular campaigns were directed at specific objectives and were quickly appeased when these goals were achieved. The Catholic Association and the Political Unions were redundant following Catholic emancipation in 1829 and the Great Reform Act in 1832. Other agitation such as the Swing movement or trade union activity was more likely to be stimulated by economic discontent and disappeared as living conditions improved. As William Cobbett observed, it wasn't easy to agitate a man 'on a full stomach'.

Popular movements did not have the leadership, organisation or arms to attempt serious revolution against a well-armed and loyal **yeomanry** and army. Indeed, with the exception of a few hotheads no popular movement actually sought revolution. Daniel O'Connell, who perhaps had the potential to mount revolutionary unrest in Ireland, believed that 'no revolution is worth the effusion of one single drop of blood'. Similarly Thomas Attwood, though commanding a large and volatile group – the Birmingham Political Union – realised that success was best achieved by keeping strictly within the law. Although reformers may have used the language of menace, their strategy was lawful and non-violent.

WHY DID THE WHIGS PASS THE GREAT REFORM ACT IN 1832?

Interpretation

Most historians agree that the Great Reform Act was a sensible concession by an enlightened parliament determined to redress the glaring inequalities in the existing electoral system. Michael Brock in *The Great Reform Act* (1973) argues that the Whig government was motivated primarily by principle and statesmanship. This view is largely accepted by Norman Gash in *Aristocracy and People* (1979) and Jack Cannon in *Parliamentary Reform 1640–1832* (1972). However Gash also argues that party political advantage to the Whigs was of importance.

E.P. Thompson in *The Making of the English Working Class* (1968) and Derek Fraser in *Popular Movements 1830-1880* (ed. J. T. Ward, 1970) argue that agitation and the threat of revolution were needed to coerce reform from a reluctant Parliament. A variant of this thesis was developed by D.C. Moore in *Victorian Studies 4* (1961) who claimed that far from conceding power, the aristocracy was determined to reinforce its privileged electoral status by a combination of deception and manipulation.

Idealism

Both Tory and Whig politicians had, since the 1780s, supported proposals for a cautious degree of parliamentary reform because of the glaring anomalies and corruption of the existing system. Reform was, however, postponed because of the revolutionary upheaval in France and because of the prolonged wars with France from 1793 to 1815. Whig leaders such as Charles James Fox and Earl Grey had been the most committed advocates of reform, arguing that the unreformed Parliament no longer reflected the growth and importance of the manufacturing interests. Rapid industrial expansion since the second half of the eighteenth century had created an affluent, ambitious and educated commercial and professional class who were still excluded from the political establishment. Their financial contribution to the defeat of Napoleon further strengthened their claim for inclusion within the constitution. The moderation, respectability and responsibility of this growing middle class particularly impressed Grey and the Whigs; indeed they appeared to share all the virtues of the landed aristocracy.

Widespread agitation

For some contemporaries, parliamentary reform was not merely a question of enlightened principle but a matter of necessity. By 1830 there was a large and sustained popular movement demanding reform. There was also widespread agitation in the southern countryside against the introduction of threshing machines, while the factory workers were protesting against low wages and rising unemployment caused by a cyclical trade depression. Although unrelated to the question of parliamentary reform, many supporters of reform were able to blame popular distress on an outdated electoral system.

Fear of revolution

Well organised and well funded political unions such as the Birmingham Political Union founded by Attwood in 1829 were able to mobilise and sustain pressure for parliamentary reform. Revolution in France in July 1830 further heightened political tension and revived memories of the horrors of 1789. Fear of political disorder no doubt encouraged some waverers in Parliament to support the Whig Bill. When the House of Lords rejected the Whig Bill in October 1831 there was widespread rioting in Nottingham, Derby and Bristol. There is no doubt that it was at this moment that England came closest to a revolutionary upheaval. Grey argued that reform was essential so as to 'avert the necessity of revolution'. Lord Macaulay urged the Lords to 'save property . . . save the multitude . . . save the aristocracy . . . the danger is terrible. The time is short'.

Self-interest

Self-interest was also a consideration in the Whig's determination to introduce the Reform Act. Grey was convinced that reform would

KEY TERM

Chandos Amendment In his amendment to the Reform Bill the Marquis of Chandos proposed that the vote be given to tenant farmers who occupied land with a rentable value of £50 a year. This amendment was passed by 232 to 148 votes. Its effect was to increase the size of the electorate but also to strengthen the electoral influence of the landowner on whom the tenant farmer relied.

strengthen, not diminish, the power of the landed aristocracy. More seats were to be given to the counties, re-drawn boundaries would ensure that more independent urban electors would not be allowed to vote in county seats, and subservient tenant-farmers would be allowed to vote with the inclusion of the **Chandos Amendment**. Moreover the Whigs realised that by allying with the manufacturing classes the political establishment would be more able to withstand challenges from the lower classes. Grey conceded that 'the middle class stands for the efficient mass of public opinion and without whom the power of the gentry is nothing'.

Party politics

While the Whigs had been for some time sympathetic to the principle of reform, they were sensitive to the growing mood in favour of reform and were quick to exploit the political advantage. It is important to look at reform in the context of the fact that the Whigs had been out of office for 40 years and that reform was popular with the manufacturing classes. They were also sensitive to the increasingly powerful and vocal national and provincial press. Support for reform was vindicated by their success in the 1830 General Election and increased by the divisions among and unpopularity of their Tory opponents.

THE IMPACT OF THE GREAT REFORM ACT

The constitutional reforms of the first half of the nineteenth century made the political system more representative and prepared the way for more radical changes later in the century. At the same time most of the traditional features of the electoral system survived. Nineteenth-century writers such as Erskine May welcomed the Great Reform Act as an essential step away from the aristocratic monopoly of power, in which Parliament was elected by a tiny electorate and in which corruption and patronage were as important as political ideals. The abolition of many pocket boroughs and the extension of the vote to the professional and commercial classes did make Parliament more open and representative. The introduction of a uniform voting qualification based upon the value of property also established a vital precedent which made further reform irresistible.

Continuity with the old political system

It is a mistake, however, to see the Whigs as far-sighted champions of political progress. The principle underlying the Reform Act was to preserve, not to destroy, aristocratic privilege. This was to be achieved by winning middle-class support and isolating radical popular reformers. It was envisaged that the Reform Act was the final settlement of the constitutional question and that a Whig–Conservative consensus would block any further political reform. Lord Grey was therefore able to claim that his act was 'essentially conservative'.

There was no change in the constitutional powers of the Crown or the House of Lords. William IV was still able to dismiss the Whig government in 1834 and the House of Lords continued to block government policy such as Home Rule for Ireland as late as 1892 and even veto budgets until 1911. To strengthen the landed interest the southern agricultural counties remained greatly over-represented: 64 more seats were given to the English counties and about 120 rotten or pocket boroughs survived. In addition, by the Chandos amendment, the vote was given to tenant farmers who could be relied upon to support their aristocratic masters. The overwhelming majority of MPs were aristocrats. Property qualifications to be an MP were set deliberately high – £600 per annum in the counties; £300 per annum in boroughs – and MPs were not paid until 1911. In any case businessmen were preoccupied in managing banks and factories and tended to limit their interests to civic politics.

Working-class leaders were bitterly disappointed by their betrayal by the middle classes. Less than one-fifth of the male adult population was able to vote after 1832 and factory workers and agricultural labourers were not fully entitled to vote until after the First World War. Even those with the vote found that only half the MPs were ever challenged in elections and that bribery and intimidation remained important elements in campaigning. Voting only became secret in 1872 and corruption remained unchecked until 1882.

Changes brought about by reform

Despite the survival of many of the old features of the political system it is important not to lose sight of the significance of the Great Reform Act. The Act was a recognition that the landed interest could no longer hope to govern without concessions to the industrial classes. The reforms of both Whigs and Conservatives clearly reflected a need for government to respond to middle-class interests. The new Poor Law and the reform of town corporations are both clear examples of the Whig sensitivity to middle-class demands. Likewise, Peel's revival of new Conservatism and his free trade policies of the 1840s were a direct appeal to the new middle-class electorate. The middle classes made advances in local government, where they won control of town councils after 1835 and played an important role in the provision of education and poor relief.

Did a two-party system emerge in the period 1815–51?

Some features of a modern **two-party system** did emerge during the first half of the nineteenth century. The Tories and Whigs of the eighteenth century were coalitions of families and factions – only loosely held

Two-party system When a government is systematically opposed by its political rivals.

together and sharing most of their ideas with their supposed political opponents, especially in their dread of French revolutionary ideals. The fierce debate stirred by the reform crisis after 1830 broke the post-war consensus and accelerated the emergence of two, more clearly defined political ideologies. Attitudes and voting on the Reform Act reflected very precisely party political affiliations. The enlarged electorate after 1832 further encouraged party political debate during election campaigns, while the need to register voters provoked the establishment of more elaborate national party organisations. Peel's direct appeal to the electorate and the defining of a party political programme in his Tamworth Manifesto in 1835 is sometimes seen as marking the rise of modern party politics.

Consensus between the parties

The politics of early Victorian England were far removed from modern conventions of politics. With the exception of the Great Reform Act, which the Conservatives accepted within three years, there was a broad consensus between the two main parties. Both Tories and Whigs supported the monarchy, the Anglican Church, landed privilege and the existing constitution. Both adopted a broadly *laissez-faire* approach to economic and social policy and both shared a fear of popular unrest and radical or democratic ideas. Most political debates ran within, not between, the two parties. Many Ultra Tories opposed Wellington's granting of Catholic emancipation in 1829; Liberal Tories such as Huskisson supported the Whigs in 1832; while 58 Whigs including Stanley, Graham, Ripon and Richmond joined Peel in opposition to the church reforms of the 1830s. The most spectacular illustration of the weakness of party discipline was the dissent within the Conservative Party after 1841. This dissent reached a crescendo in 1846 following the repeal of the Corn Laws and resulted in the division of the Conservative Party. Disraeli argued that Peel had betrayed the party, but Peel claimed that his first duty was not to the party but to the country. Many MPs continued to proclaim their independence of any party. After 1846 politics reverted to its traditional style of faction and coalitions in which personality and patronage were as important as political opinion. It was not until the 1870s that a more clearly defined party system was to establish itself.

DID A 'MODERN STATE' EMERGE IN THIS PERIOD?

State intervention

The governments of the early nineteenth century would never have envisaged the size, power and sophistication of our modern state. The reforms after 1815 did, however, reflect new political ideas. The ability of the state to wage war for 22 years demonstrated its power, while the distress of the peacetime years prompted it to take a more paternalistic approach. This is reflected in the funds for church building and public works in 1819. Likewise, the Whig reforms of the 1830s did suggest that the state was beginning to accept responsibility for the provision of education, poor relief and safety at work. It is easy to attack these measures as piecemeal and weak, but the principle established was an important one.

The role of inspectors to enforce both factory reform and educational provision was insufficient initially, but the research and evidence accumulated by the inspectors were important in generating the more radical reforms of the later nineteenth century. Moreover, the means by which reforms were devised and implemented marked a crucial modernisation of government. Driven chiefly by the campaigns of Benthamite radicals, problems such as local government, education and poverty were researched scientifically and detailed reports were published. The administration of the new Poor Law by locally elected unions accountable to a central board in London provided the blueprint of much of the reform programme ever since. The Whig reforms required that the state build an apparatus of power supported by a civil srvice with specialist knowledge. One consequence of this was the compulsory registration of births, marriages and deaths in 1836. The scope of state intervention was extended by Peel's government in the 1840s. Peel attempted to regulate the financial system by controlling banks and companies, continued to further restrict the employment of women and children and fixed the cost of rail travel and public wash houses.

Limits to state intervention

Despite the expansion in the role of the state, there were important limits to the extent that governments were prepared to intervene. The dominant political idea of the period was that of *laissez-faire*, a view first proclaimed by Adam Smith in his book *The Wealth of Nations* (1776). All governments accepted Smith's idea that wealth was best created by the unrestrained enterprise of the individual. State interference was thought to be economically damaging and corrupting to the moral fibre of working people. Political economists of the day such as David Ricardo adopted Smith's ideas without much question. It followed therefore that it was the responsibility of the individual to provide for himself and his family. **Samuel Smiles** championed the ideals of individual responsibility in his book *Self-Help* (1859). This principle was enshrined in the new Poor Law in 1834 which assumed that those in need of relief were idle or feckless. A similar approach was adopted during the Irish famine when Trevelyan opposed the release of grain from warehouses in case this encouraged prolonged dependence by the Irish peasants upon English generosity. Peel was also an ardent supporter of the principles of political economy. While he was prepared in 1844 to limit the working hours of

KEY PERSON

Samuel Smiles, 1812–1904
Author of *Self Help* published in 1859. In the book Smiles argued that the working classes should take responsibility for an improvement in their own situation. Smiles attacked the idle in society whether they were rich or poor.

women and children he strongly opposed, even by the threat of resignation, the acceptance of any restriction on the working hours of men.

HOW FAR WAS THE CHURCH REFORMED?

The extent of change

The reforms of the early nineteenth century enshrined the Anglican Church as the established religion and as such it continued to enjoy great wealth and privilege. **Disestablishment** was politically unthinkable; indeed Anglicanism even survived as the established religion of Catholic Ireland until 1869. It is important to note, however, that even the modest reforms of the Whigs to eradicate abuses stirred cries of 'the Church in danger' and led to defections by some Whigs to Peel. Gladstone conceded that he had overreacted to the church reforms. Abuses and corruption continued to be rife within the Church throughout the nineteenth century as the writer **Anthony Trollope**'s biting satire testifies. Although Catholics and nonconformists continued to suffer legal disabilities, emancipation did remove much of the sectarian poison from English politics. However, though religious observance declined and liberation increased, bigotry could still play a part in elections in cities such as Liverpool and Glasgow, especially during the debate about Home Rule for Ireland in the 1890s.

KEY PERSON

Anthony Trollope was an English novelist best known for his six 'Barchester' novels and for his six politically-based 'Palliser' novels.

CONCLUSIONS

- In attempting to adapt aristocratic rule to a more industrialised society, governments were aiming to preserve, not transform, existing institutions.
- The reforms of the first half of the nineteenth century assumed that the political world would remain elitist and that landed wealth and Anglicanism were unassailable. Social hierarchy, patronage and privilege were not threatened.
- The great majority of people were still excluded from political power. The reforms barely impinged on the lives of agricultural labourers, factory workers and women.
- At the same time it is important not to underestimate the reforms of the period. The successful challenges both to the constitution and the Church meant that further reform was unavoidable.
- The potential power of the middle classes was clearly increased and they were able ultimately to challenge vested interests.
- The state was beginning to accept that it had a responsibility to address social problems. As its expertise and income inexorably increased, the role of the state would expand. In this sense therefore it can be argued that the foundations of modern Britain were laid in the first half of the nineteenth century.

SECTION 2

Tory Men and Measures. How successful was British foreign policy, 1815–27?

KEY THEMES

- Both Canning and Castlereagh were successful in protecting British interests as they saw neccessary.
- Canning was more liberal in approach but both followed a successful foreign policy to deal with the issues that faced them.

CASTLEREAGH AS FOREIGN SECRETARY

Castlereagh's ideas
- Restoration of stability after the wars with France.
- Belief in the balance of power (or **equilibrium**) as the best means of preserving peace.
- Defence of Britain's imperial and commercial interests.
- Britain's interests could best be maintained by co-operation with its continental neighbours.

KEY THEME

Equilibrium The idea that peace is best preserved by a natural balance between states.

Viscount Castlereagh's contribution to British foreign policy during the period was significant. He was an important influence on the creation of the Congress System, protected British interests abroad and achieved reconciliation with the United States. Most important to British security was Castlereagh's work to create a 'balance of power' in Europe whereby no one country would dominate. This was mainly due to Britain's desire to avoid being involved in another war.

The Congress of Vienna
In 1815 there was some criticism in Britain of the Act of the Congress of Vienna and the fact that it restored the autocratic monarchies of Austria and Prussia with the grant of lands such as Lombardy to Austria and Danzig to Prussia. However, it is unfair to accuse Castlereagh of surrendering British national interests to the autocracies of Prussia, Austria and Russia. Their participation was important in the defeat of Napoleon and invited some territorial reward. Castlereagh actually managed to contain their territorial ambitions. The only clear underestimation was the granting of the Rhineland to Prussia. The economic resources of the area – its iron ore and coal – transformed Prussia into a major industrial power and offered an irresistible

temptation to link the two separate areas by incorporating the neighbouring states. The rise of German nationalism was to be one of the greatest threats to British interests in the second half of the nineteenth century.

Castlereagh's successes

Despite his unpopularity at home, Castlereagh was successful in achieving British objectives in foreign policy. The Act of the Congress of Vienna re-established a balance of power within Europe and laid the foundation for a century of European peace and stability. During the nineteenth century Britain was able to establish her naval, colonial and commercial supremacy throughout the world. Clearly, Britain's industrial and naval power had little to do with Castlereagh's diplomacy, but his work was vital for the growth of trade and colonial expansion made possible because Britain was able to avoid a major continental conflict. For that, Castlereagh can take some credit. At Vienna he argued successfully for the defeated France to be treated leniently. The result of this was that French ambitions in Europe were not to unsettle the balance of power. Castlereagh was the architect of the Congress System and through that was able to counterbalance the interventionist ambitions of the Holy Alliance of Russia, Austria and Prussia.

Protection of the established order

Castlereagh's main foreign policy concern was to preserve the established order in Europe. Such was the devastation of the Napoleonic wars, Castlereagh believed that the only means by which prosperity and security could be achieved was by protecting the monarchies in Austria, Prussia and Russia. Therefore, co-operation with allies in the war against Napoleon was vital to the peace and equilibrium that Castlereagh wanted to achieve. Although he disapproved of their autocratic regimes such co-operation was preferable to a revival of revolution and war. Threat of revolution was real in Europe as could be seen by the revolutions in Spain and Naples in 1820.

Conclusion

Castlereagh has been criticised for co-operating too closely with autocratic and repressive monarchies in Europe. He showed little understanding of the aims of national minorities in the Austrian, Russian or Prussian empires. He was also unsympathetic to the aims of those demanding greater political and civil liberties in Continental Europe.

However, it should be remembered that, for Castlereagh, collaborating with the other European powers did not mean accepting aspects of their foreign policy. He did prevent Russian intervention in Spain and Portugal in 1820 and he opposed Austrian intentions in Naples. What is more, Castlereagh withdrew from the Congress System when he believed that it was being used to organise joint intervention in other states. As a result he refused to sign the Troppau Protocol in 1820. It is also unfair to accuse Castlereagh of ignoring liberal and nationalist hopes. At the beginning of the century, these ideas were not always realisable. Castlereagh's achievements were many, not least the reconciliation with the United States. He had the vision to see that peaceful relations between Britain and the United States would be important to economic progress and diplomatic success over the coming years.

GEORGE CANNING

The context to Canning's foreign policy

Although more popular than Castlereagh, Canning's foreign policy had many problems. This was partly because many European and American statesmen did not trust his populist style. An example of this mistrust was the Americans' rejection of Canning's proposal for a joint statement on European interference in the affairs of American countries. Instead, the Americans issued the Monroe Doctrine in 1823. A more important reason for Canning's difficulties was the fact that, by the early 1820s, France had recovered its diplomatic self-confidence. By 1822 the anti-French alliance had been weakened. Such was its rehabilitation that the leading powers encouraged French intervention in Spain in 1823 to restore the absolute monarchy of King Ferdinand VII despite British disapproval. Nevertheless, Canning was able to deter further French intervention in Portugal or in the new states of South America.

Increasingly, the foreign policy priority of Austria, Russia and Prussia was to prevent the influence of radical movements spreading. The revolutions in Portugal and Spain in 1820 increased the determination of those such as Metternich to protect the status quo. This attitude was typified by the Carlsbad Decrees, accepted by the German Confederation in 1819, which introduced strict censorship and control of universities. In was in this context that Canning's foreign policy was made.

Canning and Russia

More serious was Canning's failure to prevent Russian expansion in the Middle East. From 1821 to 1830 the Greeks fought a war of independence against the Turkish empire. The east Mediterranean and the Balkans were strategically important for Britain as they were the gateway to the empire in the East and India. It was in Britain's interests that the Turkish empire survived and that the Russians, who were keen to extend their influence, were kept at bay. Canning, however, supported the Greeks in their war for recognition as an independent state. He attempted to set up a partnership with Russia in 1826 with the aim of influencing its actions. Under the terms of the St Petersburg Protocol,

Britain and Russia agreed to resolve the dispute between Turkey and Greece. Canning's aim was to prevent separate action by Russia. However, this policy failed. In 1827 the Turkish fleet was destroyed at the battle of Navarino by a naval expedition made up of boats from Britain, France and Russia. By then Canning was dead but the failure of policy was clear in the fact that Russia declared war against Turkey in 1828. Canning had failed to deter or persuade the Russians not to expand at the expense of the Turks. Such perceived weakness on Britain's part was one of the causes of the Crimean war in 1854.

CANNING AND CASTLEREAGH: DIFFERENCES OF STYLE OR SUBSTANCE?

Comparisons between Castlereagh and Canning are usually influenced by their strongly contrasting characters and styles.

- Castlereagh was a rather shy, reserved aristocratic statesman.
- Canning's style was much closer to that of a politician of the present. He was aware of his image and worked hard to make friends with sections of the press.

Their suspicion and dislike of each other were well known and ended in a duel in 1809.

Similarities

Despite sharp contrasts of style and character both statesmen adopted traditional principles of foreign policy. Both recognised that Britain's status as a great power rested upon a permanent peace. This could be secured by maintaining the balance of power and Britain's naval supremacy. It was Castlereagh who pushed for the foundation of the Congress System in 1815 to ensure the balance of power. Both statesmen were fully committed to the defence of trade routes and both were opposed to collective intervention in the affairs of other states. Canning failed to prevent French intervention in Spain in 1823, but Castlereagh failed to prevent Austrian intervention in Naples in 1821.

KEY THEME

Attacks on Castlereagh The poet Shelley wrote in the *Mask of Anarchy*:

I met Murder on the way
He had a mask like Castlereagh.

Castlereagh's image

It is also important not to exaggerate the ideological divisions between the two statesmen. Castlereagh's image as a reactionary politician against all change was shaped as much by his role in domestic politics as it was by his foreign policy. As leader of the House of Commons he was responsible for defending some unpopular policies such as the Coercion Acts of 1817 at a time of economic distress and social unrest. Castlereagh's poor presentation made him an **easy target to attack**. After the Napoleonic wars there was considerable anti-Tory feeling in Britain at

Peterloo in 1819. Therefore, the Whigs attacked Castlereagh as being an ally of the absolutist European powers as much because of the political climate at home. Neither politician collaborated unconditionally with the autocracies of Austria, Prussia or Russia. Similarly, Castlereagh did not intend the Congress System to become a permanent system. He worked with the other European powers as the most effective means of securing British national interests. This was vital for Britain following the destruction of the balance of power during the Napoleonic wars. As the need to contain France diminished, Castlereagh became disillusioned with the Congress System and had withdrawn from it by 1822.

Canning's objectives

Canning's approach was equally pragmatic. He was a clever politician who enjoyed his popular image at a time when many Tory politicians were hated. He was also naturally keen to exaggerate differences between his diplomacy and that of the man (Castlereagh) whom he had tried to shoot thirteen years before. Whatever the liberal element of the policies he tried to present – for example, support for Greek independence – he continued to uphold the traditional principles of foreign policy. He recognised, for example, that British commercial and strategic interests could best be served by supporting liberal regimes in Spain and Portugal and their former colonies in South America. He personally had little affection for Britain's new allies. For the New World of the Americas Canning confessed that 'as a matter of taste, I should much prefer without them'. Even the Greeks, so beloved of many liberals including the poet Byron, Canning called a 'rascally set'.

CONCLUSION

While Canning was more liberal in his approach than Castelreagh, the contrast in their foreign policies is shaped by the context in which they worked and by the style in which it was presented. Beyond this, both protected British interests.

KEY THEME

Canning's views on Britain's allies
He called the revolutionaries in Portugal who drew up the new constitution in 1822: 'the scum of the earth . . . fierce, rascally, thieving, ignorant and ragamuffins'.

SECTION 3

Tory Men and Measures. How Liberal was Liberal Toryism?

INTERPRETATION

W.R. Brock in *Lord Liverpool and Liberal Toryism, 1820–1827* (1987), argues that much of Liberal Toryism's constitutional policy was a natural continuation of its predecessors'. However, in economic policy it can be identified by its 'virtual abandonment of the agriculturists by the government and its conscious seeking after commercial support'. D. Beales in *From Castlereagh to Gladstone, 1815–1885* (1965) believes that though its foreign policy appeared more liberal, any changes after 1822 tended to be 'a greater change of style than of substance'. This line is supported by J.E. Cookson in *Lord Liverpool's Administration, 1815–1822* (1975) who argues that there was no radical shift in policy in 1822. Instead Cookson claims that 'Liverpool's administration was neither reactionary nor suddenly reformist in 1822'. This interpretation is also supported by E. Evans in the *Forging of the Modern State, 1783–1870* (1983). Evans dismisses the idea of a turning point in 1822, arguing that commercial and financial reform had been planned since 1819.

KEY THEMES

- The emergence of younger more energetic ministers after 1822 gave Lord Liverpool's government a more liberal image. This compared to the so-called Old Toryism of the first post-war ministry.
- While Lords Eldon and Sidmouth had been cautious and wary of reform, the newly promoted ministers were less so. With Robert Peel at the Home Office, Frederick Robinson at the Exchequer and William Huskisson at the Board of Trade, the government was more in touch with public opinion and more willing to accept new ideas.
- Growing prosperity and the decline in social unrest were also important in providing a more confident mood in government.
- However, in social and economic policy Liberal Toryism did not represent any departure from prevailing ideas.

CONTINUITY IN SOCIAL AND ECONOMIC POLICIES

Many of the reforms were the product of long-held ideas and were based on the work of committees set up by the previous administration. The reduction of trade tariffs in 1824 and 1828 were based upon a committee chaired by the Vice-President of the Board of Trade, Thomas Wallace, in 1820. The reduction of taxes by £12m between 1822 and 1825 was likewise only made possible by the work of the previous Chancellor Nicholas Vansittart. He had already reformed the fiscal system after 1815 and had achieved a budget surplus of £5m by 1822.

The same point can be made of Peel's reforming work at the Home Office. The centrepiece of his work, the Criminal Law Amendment Act of 1826, was recommended by the Romilly Committee set up by the Old Tories in 1819.

THE LIMITED IMPORTANCE OF REFORMS

Valuable though Liberal Tory reforms were, it is important not to overstate their importance. The achievement of a budget surplus was not so much the result of radical reordering of the fiscal system but largely due to the return to a peacetime economy and the recovery of the trade cycle. Despite the work of William Huskisson, including the Reciprocity Duties Act of 1823, most trade continued to be protected until Peel's free trade budgets of the 1840s. Indeed, in 1840 duties were still levied on 1146 articles. While the Corn Laws were amended by Huskisson's sliding scale of duties in 1828 the principle on which they rested was not seriously questioned by government for another 20 years. This supports the view that the Liberal Tories remained just as committed to the landed interests as their Old Tory predecessors.

THE EXTENT OF LEGAL AND CONSTITUTIONAL REFORM

Peel's legal reforms were wide ranging in that he ordered the revision of what had become an out-of-date Criminal Code. He reduced the number of crimes punishable by death and, in 1829, created the Metropolitan Police Force. However, Peel did not alter the principles of the Criminal Law but consolidated existing legislation. It might well be argued that the more significant moment in this period of legal reform was the decision made in 1819 to set up a Commission of Enquiry into the criminal law system. Similarly, the repeal of the Combination Laws in 1824 did not mark any radical thinking on the status of the trade unions. The suppression of combinations in 1799 and 1800 had in any case only been intended as a wartime measure. Indeed, new strict measures introduced in 1825 outlawed picketing. The legal status of the trade unions was not fully resolved during the century. It should be noted that while the Liberal Tories were prepared to introduce moderate economic and legal reforms, they, like the Old Tories, remained fundamentally opposed to institutional or constitutional reform.

THE CHANGES INTRODUCED BY LIBERAL TORYISM

While it is wrong to assume that Liberal Toryism represented any major ideological shift or inspired a series of radical reforms, it should not be dismissed out of hand. Liberal Toryism did reflect a more tolerant, imaginative and well-informed approach to social and economic problems. In some areas Liberal Tories introduced reforms of great significance. The establishment of a Metropolitan Police Force in 1829 reflected a new maturity and understanding of the causes of social unrest. By setting up a police force the government recognised that social problems could not be addressed with a combination of spies, informers and local yeomanry. Equally important were the repeal of the Test and Corporations Acts of 1828 and the granting of Catholic emancipation in 1829. By removing civil and political disabilities the Tories appeased Catholic unrest in Ireland and helped remove sectarian bitterness from English politics. Other reforms are significant not so much for their particular provisions but for the precedence they established. The modernisation of the legal system, the restoration of public finances and the liberalisation of trade all marked the beginning of a reform process which was completed by the conservative and liberal ministries of the next 50 years.

A BROADENING OF APPEAL

KEY TERM

Manufacturing interest These were the individuals who had gained a political voice through the wealth created by the new industries.

Perhaps the most significant element of Liberal Toryism was its attempt to broaden its electoral appeal by embracing the **manufacturing interest**. The return to the gold standard in 1819, which had been encouraged by Peel and Huskisson, and the amendment to the Corn Laws in 1828 were both strongly supported by manufacturers who wanted price stability to generate demand for their goods. For the landed agricultural elites these reforms signalled betrayal. Since the introduction of the Corn Laws this group expected absolute protection of wheat and enjoyed inflationary booms that secured high returns and reduced their debts. Most of the landed elite were strong supporters of the Anglican establishment and so the questions of 'Cash, Corn and Catholics' became the source of divisions between the so-called Ultra Tories and their Liberal opponents. So, while the significance of many of the reforms should not be exaggerated, the important implications of Liberal Toryism should not be overlooked. For some Tories, they represented the betrayal of Toryism. Indeed, the Conservative Party divisions of the 1840s have their roots in the rivalry between Old and Liberal Tories of the 1820s.

Conclusion

Liberal Toryism did not mark a radical change from previous Tory ideas. However it did represent the attitude of a new generation of Tory politicians.

SECTION 4

Peel and the Conservative Party, 1832–46

KEY THEMES

- The election victory of the Conservative Party in 1841 was partly due to the successful reorganisation of the party, the leadership of Peel and mistakes made by the Whigs; it should be recognised that the victory was one for traditional Tory ideas represented by 'Old Toryism'.
- Peel's ministry can be considered a success, especially considering the problems he faced. It was one of the great reforming ministries of the nineteenth century – fostering economic confidence, prosperity and a reduction of social unrest.

HISTORICAL INTERPRETATIONS

Following Norman Gash's *The Life of Sir Robert Peel* (1977), Peel has enjoyed a reputation as a shrewd political leader, an outstanding statesman and an able administrator. While many of these qualities have survived recent research, Peel's qualities as a political leader have been questioned. Most controversially, the historian Robert Blake, *Conservative Party from Peel to Thatcher* (1985), denied Peel a place as one of the great Conservative prime ministers. The reason for this was that he blamed Peel for splitting the party.

Other historians have criticised Peel for failing to transform the Conservative Party. In his article 'Sir Robert Peel and the Conservative Party: A Study in Failure' (1983) Ian Newbold argued that Peel won the 1841 election not with the ideas of the Tamworth Manifesto but with the protectionism of Old Toryism. Peel's qualities have also been questioned in a number of revisionist works including P. Adelman, *Peel and the Conservative Party* (1974) and R. Stewart, *The Foundation of the Conservative Party, 1830–1867* (1978) and *Party and Politics, 1830–1852* (1989). E.J. Evans in *The Forging of the Modern State* (1983), agrees that Peel has 'a strong claim to be considered the supreme statesman of the 19th century'.

WHY WAS THE CONSERVATIVE PARTY ABLE TO RECOVER BY 1841?

Return to the status quo

In some ways the Conservative victory in 1841 was a return to the political status quo of the 1820s. The Tory domination of the early nineteenth century was only broken by party divisions caused by Catholic emancipation and the reform crisis. Once the reform issue was settled the electorate reverted to a fundamentally conservative approach. As Lord Grey had rightly predicted, the newly enfranchised middle-class voters became champions of the political system. There was little enthusiasm for more radical reform and, as early as 1835, the Whig government was forced to depend upon Irish and radical support to maintain its parliamentary majority.

Disillusion with the Whigs

The new electorate, far from rewarding the Whigs for the vote, quickly became disillusioned with the government. This hostility was not because of the failure of the Whigs to reform but because they were seen as reflecting all the worst features of the unreformed system, that is lethargy, incompetence and, after 1839, dependence upon royal patronage for survival. Worst of all for a propertied class raised on the principles of sound finance and self-help, the government had run up a deficit of £7m by 1841. For all their championing of the interests of manufacturing in 1830, the Whigs by 1841 appeared to be elitist, lazy and wasteful.

Leadership of Peel

Peel skilfully exploited the middle-class reaction against the Whigs. In his hundred-day ministry of 1834–5 he gained support and respect for his administrative ability and statesmanship. Peel managed to distance himself from the Old Toryism of the 1830s. In the Tamworth Manifesto of 1835 Peel offered a new 'conservative' approach to politics which accepted the constitutional settlement of 1832 and promised to support the reform of proven abuses 'without infringing on established rights'. His political philosophy of constitutional stability was explained further at speeches in Glasgow in 1836 and London in 1838 and was to prove popular. Support for the idea of progressive reform and constitutional stability came from many sections of the establishment including *The Times*.

A victory for Old Toryism

However, it is misleading to suggest that the election victory of 1841 was a victory for Peel's new Conservatism. In many ways the election was a triumph of the Old Toryism of the landed classes who rallied in defence of the Anglican Church and, above all, the Corn Laws. Many landowners had been alarmed at the reforms of the Anglican Church in the 1830s, such as the Marriage Act 1836, and feared further concessions after the Whig alliance with the Irish and the radicals in 1835. More importantly, the landed classes closed ranks in defence of the Corn Laws which were considered to be essential in maintaining the prosperity of the arable farmers of southern England. Most conservative MPs were forced to give pledges to defend the Corn Laws during the campaign. It is clear that Conservative success owed much to the support of the landed interests: the party won 157 county seats as opposed to only 22 secured by the Whigs. It also did well in those boroughs small enough to allow for the landed influence to dominate. By comparison, the Conservatives made a limited impact in industrial areas, winning only a net gain of seven seats in urban constituencies with a population of over 10,000. It is clear that, for all Peel's energy and new Conservatism, among some groups the appeal of his party remained pre-Tamworth in spirit.

HOW SUCCESSFUL WAS PEEL'S 'GREAT MINISTRY', 1841–6?

Background to Peel's ministry

To assess the success of Peel's ministry it is important to remember the economic and political context. Peel became Prime Minister in 1841 at a time of economic depression, financial instability and growing popular unrest. This manifested itself in falling trade, rising unemployment and, in some areas, increasing poverty. These factors provided the background to the label the 'hungry forties'. The manufacturing classes, although now enfranchised by the 1832 Great Reform Act, resented the aristocratic grip upon Parliament as symbolised by the Corn Laws. Many in the working classes felt betrayed by what they felt was the sell-out of 1832, the imposition of the new Poor Law and the workhouses and the attack on trade union rights. Working hours remained long despite the factory legislation of the 1830s. New working-class movements including the GNCTU, the Ten-Hour movement and, above all, Chartism testified to the strength of feeling of many of the working classes. Meanwhile, Ireland remained a troubled and potentially violent land. In the light of this uncompromising background, and despite the opposition of a large faction of his own party, Peel was able to achieve a remarkable degree of success in addressing the problems he had inherited.

The restoration of stability

The main focus of Peel's ministry was the restoration of prosperity and financial stability. The near abolition of protective tariffs in 1842 and 1845 completed the work of the Liberal Tories in the 1820s and made Britain a free trade country. Given Britain's lead in manufacturing industry, the policy secured commercial prosperity throughout the nineteenth century. The value of Britain's exports nearly doubled between 1846 and 1856 as prices fell and demand increased. Peel also helped restore greater financial stability by limiting the supply of paper currency and through greater control of the Bank of England following the 1844 Bank Charter Act. Clearly, as the capital of the first industrial nation, London was able to claim a predominant status in finance. Peel's reforms ensured that its reputation was secured at a time of instability and uncertainty.

Improved social harmony
Peel was equally successful in healing some of the social tensions of the 1840s. The popular unrest of the 1840s was a reminder of the violence he had witnessed during the reform crisis in the early 1830s when he had been besieged in his own house. He believed that it was his first duty as a statesman to remove the grievances upon which social discord bred. His aim was to reconcile the working classes to existing political institutions. The budgets of 1842 and 1845 were important just as much for their social as their economic benefits. By re-introducing income tax in 1841 and by abolishing indirect taxes on a range of goods, he aimed to increase the real incomes of many of the working classes. Other legislation was aimed at improving working conditions. The 1842 Mines Act and the 1844 Factories Act regulated child and female labour; the 1844 Railway Act provided the possibility of cheap railway travel. No large-scale public health reform was passed during the time of Peel's ministry. However, significant advances were made in both awareness with the publication of Chadwick's *Sanitary Condition of the Labouring Classes* and prevention with the increase in the provision of cheap wash houses.

The repeal of the Corn Laws
For many contemporaries the most significant of Peel's reforms was the repeal of the Corn Laws in 1845. While Peel's economic philosophy provided the logic and the Irish famine the immediate cause, there is no doubt that Peel was convinced of the morality of repeal for social reasons. In his speech of 15 May 1846, Peel defended his aim to 'elevate the social character of the millions who subsist by manual labour' and claimed that he was acting upon the 'principles of equity and justice'. While the immediate economic impact of repeal can easily be exaggerated, the symbolic impact of a statesman falling from power in the defence of the interests of social justice should not be underestimated. Peel's social reforms did much to undermine Chartism which flourished on the perception of injustice.

Peel and Ireland
Peel was also willing to risk the hostility of his own party in his efforts to reconcile Catholic opinion in Ireland to the Union of 1800. Although he had established a reputation as a hard-line Protestant during his time as Irish Secretary 1812–18, 'Orange Peel', as he was nicknamed, enraged many Ultra Tories by the granting of Catholic emancipation in 1829. Throughout his time in power he continued to adopt a pragmatic policy,

upholding law and order when essential in Ireland but being prepared to recognise moderate Catholic opinion. In response to the Devon Commission of 1843 he attempted to offer compensation to tenants who had improved their holdings but the Bill was defeated by the House of Lords. Despite this, important concessions were made to Irish Catholics. Peel appointed a more sympathetic Lord Lieutenant, Lord Hartesbury; and three new colleges open to Catholics were established in Belfast, Cork, and Galway by the Irish Colleges Act of 1845. Despite the opposition of those within his party, including Gladstone who resigned from the government over the issue, the grant to the Catholic seminary at Maynooth was increased to £30,000. Peel's greatest challenge in Ireland was the onset of famine in 1845. Although his government failed to understand fully the impending catastrophe, Peel did react by signalling the end of protectionism in response to the failure of the Irish potato crop.

Failure to keep the Conservative Party united

In purely party political terms, Peel's 'great ministry' cannot be considered a success. Peel failed to convince his party of his new approach and the Conservatives experienced deep division. The party suffered a traumatic split in 1846 and was out of office for another 20 years. Peel's fall should not detract from his achievements in office. Britain was entering a period of unprecedented prosperity, government was efficient and popular agitation reduced.

WHY WERE THE CORN LAWS REPEALED IN 1846?

Key themes
* The success of the Anti-Corn Law League would appear to be self-evident as the Corn Laws were repealed within eight years of the foundation of the movement. The League did mobilise and exert pressure for repeal but this in itself does not account for success in 1846.
* The famine in Ireland made the question of the Corn Laws the most important political issue of 1846.
* The resolution of the crisis was determined by Peel who had already decided to repeal the Corn Laws for his own economic and social considerations.
* Peel's priority was to protect the agricultural interests his party represented. By the mid-1840s he believed that this section of society would be best served not by protection but by investment in the new techniques of farming which would raise productivity and compensate for any loss of earnings from falling prices.

The success of the League

The Anti-Corn Law League was one of the best-organised political movements of the nineteenth century. The clear single objective of repeal attracted many wealthy and influential middle-class supporters, especially in the north of England. The movement was led by two formidable spokesmen: Richard Cobden, who presented the case for repeal in the House of Commons and wider country with reason and clarity, and John Bright who was a passionate orator who helped give the movement a wider appeal outside Parliament. The wealth of the movement, which raised £100,000 by 1844, enabled it to sustain a powerful propaganda campaign. Pamphlets such as the *Catechism on the Corn Laws* (1827) by Colonel Thomas Perronet Thompson, *Corn Law Rhymes* (1830) by Ebenezer Elliot and the *Anti-Corn Law Circular* were distributed nationwide, thanks to the induction of the penny post in 1840. In addition, *The Economist* championed the cause of reform. The League also organised lectures, meetings and bazaars to spread the message and raise funds. The Free Trade Hall with a capacity of 8000 was opened in Manchester in 1843. The League was able to win parliamentary support by buying up freeholds to win by-elections. Cobden was elected as an MP in 1841, Bright in 1843. Peel certainly recognised the influence of the League in Parliament. After hearing Cobden's speech in March 1845, putting forward the case for repeal, **Peel conceded the logic of the case against the Corn Laws.**

KEY THEME

Peel's attitude in 1845 After hearing Cobden, Peel turned to Sidney Herbert, commenting: 'You must answer this for I cannot.'

Limits to the League's success

The success of the Anti-Corn Law League should not, however, be overstated. While the League did attract strong support in the new industrial towns of the north, its impact in London was limited and it failed to win any support from tenant farmers and agricultural labourers. Similarly, many industrial workers saw the League's campaign as an attempt to reduce wages. Its influence also fluctuated with economic conditions. With increasing prosperity and a succession of good harvests 1842–4 enthusiasm for the movement declined. Moreover, Peel's modification of the sliding scale in 1842 and a well-organised protectionist counterattack challenged the League's case. Cobden and Bright converted few fellow MPs and the annual vote to repeal was decisively rejected.

The importance of the famine

Therefore, despite the activity of the League, the question of repeal was not seriously considered until the Irish famine of 1845. While it is clear that repeal of the Corn Laws would have no immediate effect on resolving the famine, Peel recognised the moral and political difficulty of taxing food imports at a time when many in Ireland were dying of starvation. Suspension of the laws was ruled out as this would concede the League's case and might force Peel to reintroduce them in an election year. The greatest opposition to repeal, however, was from among the ranks of his own party.

Peel's conversion to free trade

Peel had become converted to the case for repeal before the Irish famine. This was partly because of the self-evident success of the abolition of protective tariffs on manufactured goods. To put it simply, Peel became convinced that, like industry, agriculture would not only survive but flourish in a free trade market. The repeal of the Corn Laws was accompanied by a customs law, which abolished duties on foodstuffs, and a drainage grant. His modification of the sliding scale in 1842 is a reflection of his conversion to the principle of free trade. He was, by 1842, a free trader who planned to educate his party.

Repeal for reasons of social harmony

Peel recognised the moral argument in favour of repeal. He hoped that by challenging landed privilege and reducing the cost of food he would reconcile the working classes to aristocratic government. Peel was alarmed by the popular agitation of the 1840s and feared a return to the mob violence of 1831 and 1832 when his own home had been besieged. Although Peel was opposed both to conceding the vote and to regulation of the working hours for men, he was convinced that it was essential for government to address the grievances of those people who were 'brought into no direct relationship by the exercise of the elective franchise'. By repealing the Corn Laws and raising the living standards of the working classes, Peel hoped to remove further demands for constitutional change. In his resignation speech of 29 July 1846, Peel defended repeal which, he believed, offered workers 'abundant and untaxed food, the sweeter because it is no longer leavened by a sense of injustice'. However it should be noted that Peel refused to concede either the vote or factory reform. He personally intervened to block the ten hour legislation.

Conclusions

- It is clear, therefore, that for all its wealth and organisation, the Anti-Corn Law League was not powerful enough to bring about the repeal of the Corn Laws.
- The Corn Laws were repealed partly because of the Irish famine but chiefly because Peel had become convinced not only of their irrelevance but their social divisiveness.
- After 1841 Peel had determined that it was his duty as a statesman to repeal them.

WHY DID THE CONSERVATIVES SPLIT IN 1846?

Key themes
- The immediate cause of the Conservative split in 1846 was Peel's decision to repeal the Corn Laws following the famine in Ireland.
- In many ways, however, this crisis was the culmination of years of conflict between Peel and a large faction of his party, not only during his great ministry but throughout most of his leadership of the party since 1834. This conflict was made greater by personal antagonism and the opportunism of Benjamin Disraeli.
- The split was the climax of the debate over protectionism which had been taking place within the party for some time.

Opposition to repeal
Peel's decision to repeal the Corn Laws was opposed by two-thirds of his party and his fate was therefore sealed. For many Conservatives the Corn Laws were essential to protect, not only their incomes, but their status. Repeal, therefore, not only threatened their incomes by reducing the price of wheat but challenged the foundations of the social and political order. Many Conservative MPs had promised to defend the Corn Laws in the election of 1841: to them repeal was a betrayal of the party's pledges. For the Ultra Tories Peel had betrayed the party just as he had done over Catholic emancipation in 1829.

Peel's style of leadership

KEY THEME

Peel's relationship with Queen Victoria
In 1841 Greville observed that Peel's attitude to Queen Victoria reminded him of the attitude of 'a dancing master giving a lesson'.

Clearly, Peel's position in 1846 was bound to be difficult. His vulnerability was made worse by his personal isolation within the party. The landed elite within the Conservative Party were suspicious of Peel and shared **Queen Victoria's dislike** of his seriousness. In power Peel's autocratic style alienated some of his supporters. Rather than form a cabinet which reflected the different factions within his party he selected a group of like-minded colleagues, a 'cabinet of dolls' as Lord Ashley complained. He demanded absolute loyalty and failed to compromise. He threatened to resign if a 'Ten Hours' amendment proposed by rebel backbenchers were accepted as part of the Factory Bill in 1844. Again in 1844, over the issue of the duty paid on sugar, Peel was resentful and unforgiving against those in his own party, including the backbencher P. Miles, who promoted the idea of imperial preference. Many of his measures after 1841 were likely to alienate backbenchers but Peel's bloody-mindedness and indifference served to intensify opposition. After the sugar debate and Peel's attack on those who opposed him from within the party, William Gladstone remarked: 'A great man has committed a great error'.

The role of Disraeli
Peel's unpopularity was skilfully exploited by his rival Benjamin Disraeli.

Denied a position in cabinet in 1841, Disraeli pursued a political vendetta against Peel. At the same time, Disraeli also appealed to disaffected Tories by his '**Young England**' movement which challenged the values of industrial society. Disraeli attacked Peel as 'middleman', the politician who had betrayed Conservative principles. In the highly charged atmosphere on the Conservative Party back benches in the early 1840s, Disraeli's criticisms won support. Most importantly, Disraeli managed to transform the defence of the Corn Laws from one of greed and self-interest to a noble cause in defence of principle. The personal antagonism between Disraeli and Peel undoubtedly added to the crisis of 1846.

KEY TERM

Young England A group of aristocratic Tories who wished for a return to traditional Tory values.

Fundamental divisions

At the heart of Conservative divisions was the fundamental conflict of ideas which had troubled the party since the late 1820s. Peel had been a leading Liberal Tory after 1822 and believed that the party should attempt to appeal to a constituency beyond the landed elite. This was shown in the Tamworth Manifesto of 1835. His support for currency reform and free trade reflected his conviction that government should be responsive to the interests of the new industrial classes. Similarly, his acceptance of the need for Catholic emancipation, although prompted by the threat of unrest in Ireland, was a further attempt to abandon the Protestant bigotry of Old Toryism. To the Ultra Tories, however, the three great questions of 'Cash, Corn and Catholics' revealed Peel to be a traitor to the Anglican Church and the landed interest. The Old Tories may have accepted Peel as their leader in 1834 because they recognised that no one could have so successfully engineered their return to power by 1841. The old guard wanted his leadership but not his ideas. Despite its electoral appeal, many Tories were not reconciled to Peel's moderate reformism outlined in his Tamworth Manifesto. This ideological debate poisoned relations between Peel and many backbenchers throughout his great ministry. Peel's abolition of duties on cattle (1842), Canadian corn (1843) and sugar (1844) were further evidence of the abandonment of the landed interest. At the same time his concession to Irish Catholics, particularly the Maynooth grant, were regarded as proof of Peel's treachery. Even before the Corn Law crisis, therefore, large numbers of Conservative backbenchers were already prepared to destroy Peel.

The nature of Parliament

The crisis within the Conservative Party also reflected a conflict about the nature of Parliament itself. First and foremost Peel saw himself as a servant of the Crown with the duty to serve the national interests over and above those of the party. This was the traditional view of the role of the Prime Minister and was sharpened in Peel's case by his contempt for many within his own party. However, Peel's problem was that the influence of political parties was increasing. The Great Reform Act had sharpened the ideological conflict between parties; the expansion of the electorate to urban areas and the need to register voters had bolstered the role of party machines. A long period of opposition had further consolidated Conservative forces in reaction against Whig radicalism. Ironically, Peel's own Tamworth Manifesto also seemed to highlight the growing loyalty towards party principles.

Conclusion

The Conservative Party split in 1846 occurred because the party had failed to come to terms with deep internal ideological differences. The crisis was heightened by Peel's own arrogance and aloofness but the root of the problem was his determination to serve what he viewed as the interests of the nation at the expense of narrow party-political self-interest.

SECTION 5

Radicalism and the state: the Chartist experience

INTRODUCTION

The causes of Chartism are central to explaining its nature and decline. The debate revolves around whether Chartism was a product of the economic and social forces of the time or whether it was stimulated by political forces. Before reading this section you should read Chapter 10 (pages 79–90) in the AS section of the book.

HISTORICAL INTERPRETATION

The argument that Chartism was mainly caused by economic and social distress was first put forward by contemporary writers such as Thomas Carlyle and J.R. Stephens who, in 1838, described the issue of universal suffrage as a 'knife and fork' question. Carlyle believed that Chartism was a social phenomenon, its 'living essence ... the wrong disposition of the working class'. Similarly, the novelist Mrs Gaskell saw Chartism in terms of anger, distress and the breakdown of social relationships, mainly because of the effects of industrialisation. The German writer F. Engels witnessed the impact of the Chartist movement in the late 1830s and early 1840s. He believed that Chartism was a working-class movement created by the new relationships of production. This contemporary view has been backed by historians including F.C. Mather who wrote that 'most people who entered Chartism did so to rectify some social injustice'.

Similarly, there have been many attempts to link the fortunes of local Chartist groups to their economic environment. F.C. Mather has tried to show that Chartism was strongest in areas with a depressed economy; for example outworkers and hand loom weavers in Lancashire and those living in medium-sized industrial towns such as Stockport which were affected by the depression at the end of the 1830s. A. Briggs argued that Chartism was the product of industrialisation and the growth in communication which enabled a local movement to become a national one.

One of the most influential writers in the debate about the origins of Chartism has been the economist W.W. Rostow. In his explanation of how the nineteenth-century economy worked, Rostow showed how the early industrial economy was characterised by swings in the trade cycle. Rostow tried to show that there was a link between troughs in the trade cycle and social unrest such as the outbreaks of Chartism in 1839, 1842 and 1848. This line of thought was developed by A. Briggs. He argued that economic depression led to despair among the less prosperous such as the hand loom weavers or the framework knitters of Leicestershire, Nottinghamshire and the east Midlands. These groups' demands for better wages and working hours led Briggs to quote Carlyle: 'food, shelter, due guidance in return for his labour – candidly interpreted, Chartism and all such isms meant that'.

In contrast to the line of argument which identifies Chartism as a movement born out of economic and social problems is the belief that one can place Chartism in the context of political factors. In *The Making of the English Working Class* (1963) E.P. Thompson argued that Chartism was a radical movement based on political ideology – the response to the political exclusion of the working classes by the Reform Act of 1832 and the nature of the Whig reforms of the 1830s which followed. The historian G. Stedman Jones has tried to show that Chartism emerged as a protest against the political system and the exclusion of the majority from that system. Stedman Jones accepted that Chartism was diverse and had many forms of local expression but it was adherence to the Charter which made Chartism a mass movement. To Stedman Jones 'political power is the cause [of Chartism]'.

KEY THEMES

- The economic and social distress of the 1830s and 1840s should be seen as the wider context in which Chartism developed.
- Economic distress does not adequately explain why the discontent of the period was expressed in the form of the Charter.
- The identity of Chartism as a movement based on radical ideals gave it its coherence.

WHAT WERE THE POLITICAL ORIGINS OF CHARTISM?

Radical background
From the 1770s to 1790s, radicals such as Thomas Paine in *The Rights of Man* criticised the corrupting effects of the concentration of political power in the hands of an elite few. The Whigs had raised the hopes of the working classes but they were to be disappointed by the reforms of the 1830s. The Great Reform Act of 1832 gave the vote to the middle classes but not the working classes. Most importantly, the new Poor Law

of 1834 reinforced the radical view that only political reform would end injustice: 'we will never unshackle labour from its misery until the people possess that power under which all oppression and monopoly must cease' (Charter, 1842). The six points of the Charter, and the demand for universal suffrage in particular, represented a critique of the established order. Behind the demands was the belief that working people should control their own destiny.

Discontent with the Whigs

There is much evidence in Chartist literature of discontent with the Whig legislation of the 1830s. The new Poor Law was widely despised for introducing a system of 'moral imprisonment'. The manifesto of the 1839 National Convention asked: 'will you permit the stroke of affliction, the misfortunes of poverty and the infirmities of age to be branded and punished as crimes?' Despite the divisions among the Chartists over tactics, between those who supported the use of physical force led by Feargus O'Connor and moral force led by William Lovett, there remained a shared radical critique of society. The central theme of Lovett's book *State and Condition of the Millions* (1841) was that the success of the Charter would lead to an end of oppression. To many in the Chartist movement, a widening of the franchise would bring legislation that would represent the working classes' true interests, such as a Ten Hours Act and the end to transportation of trade unionists.

The nature of Chartist grievances

Despite the diversity of the Chartist movement there is evidence that there was a basic grasp of the meaning of the Charter. For example, the Knaresborough Working Men's Association in 1839 wrote: 'it appears to us quite evident that the primary cause of all the evils under which we labour is class legislation'. The south Lancashire Chartists did not see the Charter as the means by which their economic position could be immediately improved. Instead, they saw it as a means by which they could gain political power. In the *English Chartist Circular* of 1842 they wrote: 'nothing short of political power to protect our labour will satisfy us, the working calls of this country'. Although the 1842 Charter speaks of economic grievances the ultimate cause of those grievances was the political structure. When the ruled were given the vote, argued the Chartists, then these grievances could be dealt with.

Relations with the Anti-Corn Law League

It was the discontent with the Whigs and their legislation which helps to explain the absence of an alliance with the middle-class radicals in the Anti-Corn Law League. Although repeal of the Corn Laws was in the economic interest of the working classes, there was no support from the Chartists for the Anti-Corn Law League. They did not see repeal in the interests of the working class. They felt any benefit in terms of reducing bread prices would be lost in corresponding wage cuts. For this reason Chartism received little support from the middle classes. Many middle-class members of the Chartist movement such as Thomas Attwood or the Reverend J.R. Stephens eventually left the movement because they could not accept the idea of universal male suffrage. There were attempts by middle-class radicals to form an alliance with Chartists. However, they failed because of the fundamental and deep-seated divisions between those who had political power and those who did not. An example of such an attempt which failed was the Complete Suffrage Union formed in 1842 by Joseph Sturge, a merchant from Birmingham. While accepting the six points, Sturge refused to accept the name 'People's Charter' for the movement's programme. At a Complete Suffrage Union conference in December 1842, William Lovett and Feargus O'Connor joined forces to propose that the Charter be accepted in name. The proposition was accepted and the distinct nature of Chartism as a working-class movement was preserved.

Self-help

A very important aspect of Chartism were the ideas of self-help and self-improvement. Chartist schools were set up with the aim of teaching democratic values and principles. The Chartist newspaper set up by Feargus O'Connor, the *Northern Star*, combined militant politics with an improvement ethic. Its sub-editor Harney wrote 'knowledge is power; and the result of its present widespread diffusion must be the political, and ultimately the social emancipation of the masses'. In 1841 Thomas Cooper set up an adult education school in Leicester with the aim of self-improvement.

Different Chartist groups

There were many different forms of Chartist expression. However, despite their differences, all Chartists shared the perception of oppression. A good example was the Christian Chartist movement which attacked the privileges of the Established Church of England. In 1840 and 1841 Chartist churches were set up in which the elements of Christianity which stressed democracy were preached. The new Poor Law was attacked by the Christian Chartists with the argument that it dissolved God-given marriage bonds by splitting up the sexes in workhouses. Attacks on the Church of England were very much in the spirit of the Charter. The editor of the *Northern Star* until 1843, the Reverend William Hill, stressed the link between Christianity and Chartism. He wrote of 'the principles of social benevolence and justice, of civil equality and of political right ... [as] recognised by the Bible'. It was the Church of England which represented the idle, the established, the oppressor.

Key themes
- To many historians the Chartist movement has appeared divided. In particular, there appeared to be a division in the leadership of the movement between those who favoured the use of moral force, led by William Lovett, and those who preferred physical force, led by Feargus O'Connor. This line of argument was established in the 1850s, particularly through the work of R.G. Gammage whose *History of the Chartist Movement* attacked O'Connor's leadership in particular.
- However, it is also possible to argue that the diversity of Chartism gave it its strength. While accepting that Lovett and Harney, for example, might be different in terms of political temperament, they shared the belief that implementation of the Charter would bring about change.

Lovett and O'Connor
The interpretation that the differences between O'Connor and Lovett highlight a divided movement can be challenged. It is acceptable to argue that they were very different characters within what should be seen as a broad church. But they both adhered to the Charter and they both accepted the tactic of parliamentary petition as the best means by which the political rights of the working people could be achieved. The characterisation of O'Connor as a man of violence is rather too simplistic. He recognised that uprising would be futile and in 1839 distanced himself from the Newport rising. Although he spoke in uncompromising terms in 1842 about the need for Chartists to arm themselves, this should be placed more in the context of a period in which the bearing of arms was common. It is therefore simplistic to label O'Connor as a 'physical force' Chartist. Both Lovett and O'Connor agreed on the main methods of campaigning, that of Conventions and mass-meetings as well as the petitions. Although the *Northern Star* was set up by O'Connor, it was the newspaper for the whole movement and O'Connor gave its editors such as Harney considerable editorial freedom.

Where Connor and his critics, who included Lovett, split was on the tone of the movement. After his release from prison in 1841, Lovett turned away, not from the Charter, but from the type of movement envisaged by O'Connor. The historian D. Thompson neatly sums up the relationship between the two by saying 'Lovett and the LWMA represented not so much an alternative leadership to the Chartist movement, as a different sort of movement altogether'. The National Charter Association founded in 1841 was not to the taste of those Chartists whose roots were more in the radicalism of the London artisans (such as Lovett) rather than the mass following of sections of the urban working classes. Hence Lovett's 'new move' in 1841 to look for a solution through education. However, it should be stressed that both adhered to the centrality of the Charter to their cause. When Joseph Sturge's Complete Suffrage Union attempted to woo Lovett in 1842 he rejected the initiative and sided with O'Connor in criticising its intentions. Both mistrusted the middle classes, especially in the light of the failure of the working classes to be granted the vote in 1832. Most importantly, both Lovett and O'Connor were radicals. They shared the same radical critique that the majority in Britain were oppressed because they were excluded from political power.

While O'Connor damned Lovett's 'education Chartism' there is a similarity between it and the idealism of O'Connor's land plan. Both projects recognised the element of self-improvement necessary to prepare the working classes for political power. It has been argued that the land plan was misguided and shows O'Connor's recklessness. Again, this is not the case. As with the 'new move' the land plan had its roots in radical thought. Much of William Cobbett's *Rural Rides* written earlier in the century focused on the issue of land. The Land Company's popularity showed the strength of the Chartist ethos and the flexibility of the movement.

WHY DID CHARTISM FAIL AND DECLINE?

If one argues that Chartism was a reflection of the Whigs' rule in Britain in the 1830s then real reform or perceived change to the system undermined the Chartist movement. The 'class legislation' of the 1830s, for example, the new Poor Law, was not repeated in the 1840s. Instead, Peel in particular introduced legislation that was less oppressive: the Mines Act of 1842 was followed by the repeal of the Corn Laws in 1846, a Ten Hours Act in 1847 and the abolition of the hated Poor Law Commission in 1847. Chartism began to fail as a coherent critique of the political system when the urgency for political change became less apparent in the eyes of its supporters. The significance of Peel's legislation was that it loosened the link between the oppression of the working classes and the monopoly of political power. It was this factor rather than an improvement in economic conditions which led to the decline of Chartism.

Opposition to Chartism
There is little doubt that the forces deployed by the state to control Chartism were most effective. The state used repression and propaganda in order to protect the status quo. If one argues that Chartism was a coherent political force, then the roots of its decline must lie not in the movement itself but in the determination of its opponents. The political establishment in Britain had far wider support than many of the continental states. This was partly due to the impact of the 1832 Reform Act which enfranchised the middle classes and isolated those who

demanded working-class enfranchisement. On top of this, successive governments showed themselves tactically flexible but resolute in dealing with Chartism.

Use of repression

When necessary the police and army dealt most effectively with serious Chartist disturbances. They were aided in their effectiveness by the new railways which helped move the police and troops around the country at speed. Examples of the effective use of repression are many. In 1842 the strikes inspired in the Potteries by Thomas Cooper led to an outbreak of violence and attacks on property. The authorities used the army to control the extent of the uprising and end the unrest. Equally illuminating was the reluctance of the authorities to use the death penalty against Chartists. After the Potteries uprising over 200 people were either transported or imprisoned. The significance of this was that the authorities avoided making martyrs, instead preferring to isolate the Chartist leadership. This was also the case in 1839–40. In the wake of the Newport rising three Chartists – including the leader John Frost – were sentenced to death. All, however, were pardoned on the appeal of presiding judge Chief Justice Tindal who recognised the folly of inflaming the Chartist cause further.

Perhaps the best example of the effectiveness of the authorities in thwarting the Chartists was in 1848. The whole Kennington Common episode highlighted the significance of middle-class action. The organisation of a demonstration to present the Third Petition had resulted in the calling up of special constables by the Home Secretary the Duke of Wellington. By the day of the Kennington Common meeting on 10 April the special constables numbered 85,000 and they were backed up by a force of 12,000 police and soldiers. Against such a force the Chartists had little choice but to accept the advice of the Superintendent of the Metropolitan Police that the petition could be carried to Parliament by a small group. There are questions as to whether the 1848 Chartists represented a real threat to the established order. However, that is not the issue. The opposition of the middle classes to Chartism and their willingness to support repressive although not overly repressive measures to deal with the movement limited its chance of success.

The impact of Chartism

Impact on political events. It is important not underestimate the impact Chartism had on politicians at the time. However, it was only one of many movements that highlighted what the writer Thomas Carlyle called the 'Condition of England Question'. The Ten-Hours movement, Anti-Corn Law League, the Complete Suffrage Union and others brought to the attention of politicians such as Sir Robert Peel the distress felt nationwide. However the importance of Chartism was that it spelt out most clearly the concerns and political aspirations of the majority. There is little doubt that Peel's conversion to free trade in the 1840s was partly conditioned by his desire to remove the obvious signs of oppression, the Corn Laws, and with them high prices. He also hoped, through the 1841 and 1843 budgets to usher in an era of prosperity that would reduce the calls for working class suffrage.

Similarly Chartist agitation highlighted a move of discontent that eased the passage of social legislation such as the Factory Act of 1844. Another significant aspect of Chartism was its encouragement of working class literacy and education. However widespread, education for the working class was perceived as much of a threat by the churches and State as was political emancipation. State involvement in education developed as the century progressed but even important legislation such as Forster's Education Act in 1870 fell short of providing an adequate education for all. In 1867 the franchise was widened to include some members of the working class, by the Second Reform Act.

Limitations of Chartism. At the same time the impact of Chartism should not be exaggerated. It is the case that five out of the six points of the Charter were implemented in the 80 years that followed Chartism: property qualifications for MPs were scrapped in 1859, the secret ballot was introduced in 1871, MPs were paid from 1911 and equal electoral districts and working-class franchise was extended to some urban workers in 1867 and to agricultural labourers in 1885. However, although Chartism provided a political education for many sections of the working class, it is difficult to ascribe the introduction of these factors directly to Chartism. Indeed, the success of the Anti-Corn Law League in securing the passage of repeal of the Corn Laws in 1846 or the Ten-Hour Movement in 1847 stand in stark contrast to the lack of movement on the issue of political representation within the lifetime of many of Chartism's leaders and its supporters.

CONCLUSION

- Economic distress was the context in which Chartism flourished. It was at its heart a political movement.
- Political change reduced support for Chartism.
- While a significant movement at the time, the impact of Chartism should not be exaggerated.

SECTION 6

What was the extent of economic change, 1815–51?

KEY THEMES

- In agriculture the period was not one of universal stagnation. One sees distress in certain areas in the wake of the Napoleonic wars but also innovation and change driven by the growth in population and protection.
- The idea of an 'industrial revolution' in the period 1820–51 has to be challenged. There were changes in technology but their impact was gradual and not sudden. This period should be seen as one of significant continuity in economic development alongside dramatic change in select areas.

WHAT WAS THE SIGNIFICANCE OF POPULATION GROWTH, 1820–51?

Importance in creating demand

The growth in the population during this period in Great Britain was to be of fundamental significance. It influenced the growth of agriculture and industry through an increase in demand for their goods of around one-third. The expanding domestic market was the key to the growth of the economy between 1820 and 1851. It also shaped the level of technological change. A rapidly expanding and younger population reduced the drive for innovation because of the abundant supply of cheap labour available to employers. In many industries the challenge for producers was to meet the increase in demand by using established technology but on a greater scale; examples of this can be seen in the iron, coal and, to an extent, textile industries.

Changes in employment patterns

The population growth of the period changed the age structure of Britain. Those termed dependants – either aged 0–15 or 60 plus – increased from 700 per 1000 in 1750 to 850 per 1000 in the 1820s. In England between 1806 and 1836 there were more children under 15 than there were adults aged 25–59. This had a significant impact on the economy; for example, the increase in the use of child labour which was cheap and readily available. In 1835 Andrew Ure pointed out that in the Lancashire cotton industry, adult men on average earned 22s 8½d a week whereas children earned 4s 10¾d a week. Therefore, employers were encouraged to use child labour; in the late 1830s, 29 per cent of workers in the cotton industry were under the age of 18.

The extent of migration

The migration of population to work in productive sectors of the economy was crucial to the growth of both population and industry. Therefore, the population growth provided a dynamic for industrial change, and the two factors were very closely linked. However, the nature of industrial change was not dramatic enough to cause new patterns of population mobility. Migration was mainly local; for example, in Preston in 1851, 70 per cent of immigrants came from within a 30-mile radius of the town. It was not until the mid-nineteenth century that there was depopulation of certain rural areas. From the 1840s Wiltshire suffered a population loss, to be followed by counties such as Cambridgeshire and Norfolk in the 1850s. This suggests that until the middle of the century the pull factors of industrial change and the push factors of agricultural change were not strong enough to radically alter the population structure.

WHAT ARE THE KEY FACTORS IN EXPLAINING THE EXTENT OF AGRICULTURAL CHANGE?

The extent and impact of agricultural change during the period in question relies very much on geographical location. The extent of the depression in agriculture has been exaggerated because of the over-reliance on sources produced by those hardest hit. Most famous of the evidence backing the image of widespread depression was Lord Ernle's *English Farming Past and Present* (published in 1912). **Ernle described a bleak picture**.

The reliability of the evidence

However, Ernle largely relied on the testimony of wheat farmers who had given evidence to the Board of Agriculture in 1816 and parliamentary commissions in 1821, 1833 and 1836, investigating levels of rural distress. These farmers were intent on painting the worst picture with the aim of gaining compensation and greater protection from the government. Similarly, Cobbett's picture in *Rural Rides* should be treated with suspicion as he was an outspoken supporter of the need for further protection of agriculture.

The problems associated with heavy soils

It should be argued that the heavy soil farmers who did suffer from the price deflation of the 1815–36 period had been unnaturally protected from the competition of their light soil rivals by the Napoleonic wars. Those who were able to innovate prospered in this period. Despite the

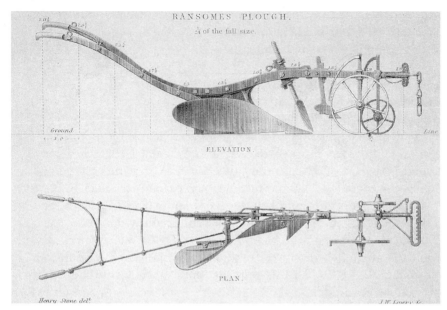

ELEVATION.

PLAN.

Henry Stone del.ᵗ   J.W. Lowry G.

Ransome's plough.

fall in prices, many farmers were able to increase their yield by introducing new farming techniques. The information on these techniques was widely available; for example, in 1828 the *Quarterly Journal of Agriculture* was first issued. Innovators such as William Youatt and Justus von Liebig wrote popular books on issues as diverse as grazing and fertilisers. The Napoleonic wars (1793–1815) and the subsequent rise in wheat prices had encouraged farmers to grow wheat. With a fall in prices, those in areas where other forms of farming were the norm reverted to traditional production. In the 1820s and 1830s in Leicestershire, dairy and pasture farming predominated. In areas such as Lancashire and Cheshire in which there was dramatic urban expansion, and therefore a growth in the demand for dairy and other goods, farmers barely suffered. Many areas saw a greater tendency to mixed farming, arable and pasture together. The fodder crop of the four-crop rotation which could be used on light soils was fed to livestock whose dung could be used as fertiliser to improve arable yield.

Innovation in agriculture
The extent of innovation and change can be seen in the fact that from 1801 to around 1851 the amount of cropland growing root crops grew from 11 per cent to 20 per cent. While all prices fell, those of goods such as wool and malting barley were far more stable than wheat. Indeed, with the abolition of beer duties in 1830, the demand for barley rocketed. The 1830s and 1840s should be considered as periods in which the use of machinery became widespread. Ransome of Ipswich flourished as the leading manufacturer of iron ploughs and other tools suitable for sandy

soils. Similarly, yields were boosted by the use of imported fertiliser such as guano. So it is wrong to characterise the period as one of universal stagnation. The engine of agricultural growth was the population growth which encouraged and rewarded investment in innovation while agriculture basked under the umbrella of protection from the Corn Laws. Indeed, it is in this period that one sees the roots of high farming which is usually associated with agriculture after 1851.

There was some necessary readjustment in rural England in the first half of the century which had a negative impact on communities. By 1820 the enclosure of land was virtually complete but many farms were small and their farmers could not afford to innovate. Those who farmed on the cold clay lands of the Midlands and parts of East Anglia could not innovate to the same extent because the soils were unsuitable for such a purpose. Of particular concern was the fact that heavy soils were unsuitable for fodder crops such as turnips and the three-crop rotation continued to be used with the wheat crop used as the cash crop. Here was the problem, for with the collapse in wheat prices came the high levels of distress as voiced by Lord Ernle and Cobbett. However, not only did arable prices pick up again after 1837 but the introduction of cheap drainage tiles and clay drains in the 1840s led to the proper drainage of heavy lands. The impact for those who invested was considerable in that it allowed the farmer to forgo the fallow year.

HOW SIGNIFICANT WAS THE DEVELOPMENT OF THE FACTORY SYSTEM, 1820–51?

The idea of an **industrial revolution** during the period 1820–51 has to be challenged. There were changes in technology, such as Watt's steam engine or Cartwright's power loom, but their impact was gradual and not sudden. The growth of large-scale factory production was limited to the textile industries and cotton in particular.

Since Rostow, various historians and economists have argued that Britain experienced far more gradual economic growth. In *British Economic Growth during the Industrial Revolution* (1985) N.F.R. Crafts argued that the rate of growth in the economy was relatively modest. Whereas some industries such as cotton and iron experienced dynamic growth, they were exceptions rather than the rule.

Textiles

Between 1820 and 1851 factories existed in a partnership with the domestic system, not independent of it. Much employment in industry by 1851 continued to be in small-scale, handicraft industries. Growth in many industries was relatively slow. In a few industries, investment in

KEY TERM

Industrial revolution In *The Unbound Prometheus* (1969) the historian David Landes defined the term 'industrial revolution' as the change from 'an agrarian, handicraft economy to one dominated by industry and machine manufacture'. In *The Stages of Economic Growth* (1960), W.W. Rostow suggested that Britain had experienced economic take off which resulted in 'a decisive transition' towards an economy dominated by industry.

factories and new technology meant that British industry was able to dominate its competitors. However, it should be reiterated that this was only part of the overall picture of industrial development and that there was significant continuity in terms of methods of production and employment.

Continuity in textiles. It is with the manufacture of textiles that the factory system is most closely associated. The advances in the production of cotton are without doubt. However, it is wrong to overemphasise the advancement in technology. Innovations such as Samuel Crompton's mule and Edmund Cartwright's power loom were significant in that they marked an important stage in the shift to larger scale production. However, many such innovations were simply refinements of existing technology; for example the mule was an amalgamation of the spinning jenny and the water frame. The important changes during the period in question were in the refinements of the recent innovations. The reason for this was simple: much of the new technology was technically flawed and ill-suited to producing quality goods on a large scale. Therefore, the significant changes were made by those such as Richard Roberts and Henry Maudsley who, in the early 1820s, designed a self-acting mule which made it more appropriate for factory use. The power loom was even more unreliable as it placed too great a strain on the yarn. It took Roberts and William Horrocks to refine the power loom but one should argue that it was not until the 1830s that its use became widespread. The period saw a significant shift to the use of steam power; by the mid-1830s steam was used in around three-quarters of textile production and by 1850 nine-tenths of cotton mills were steam powered. However, this relied on adaptation of James Watt's rotary steam engine which meant that the machine's efficiency quadrupled from 1800 to 1850. The key point to make is that technology evolved in the period and the factory system was introduced gradually.

Increasing productivity. There is no doubt that this new technology improved productivity: from 1780 to 1860 the cotton industry's productivity grew at 2.6 per cent per year. Innovation also laid the basis for the boom in cotton production; exports of cotton piece goods rose from 227 million yards in 1810–19 to 978 million yards in 1840–9. It also dramatically reduced the cost of cotton cloth: a piece selling in the 1780s for 80 shillings would cost around 5 shillings in the 1850s. The innovations considerably reduced the cost of producing cotton cloth. Other textile industries such as wool and worsted lagged behind the advances made by cotton for the reason that the yarns were not well suited to the new mechanised process. Much factory-based manufacturing in these industries was based on preparation and finishing of goods. The table based on factory returns is most instructive.

Textile mills in Britain, 1850

	Cotton	Woollen	Worsted	Flax	Silk	Total
No. of mills	1921	1488	499	324	277	4509
No. of workers (000s)	329.2	73.9	79.7	47.3	42.6	572.7
Average workers per mill	171	50	160	146	154	127

(Source: D. Jenkins, *REFRESH*, issue 16, Spring 1993, p. 2.)

The factory returns show that even in the most technologically advanced sector of the economy – textiles – many still did not work in factories. The 1851 census counted 537,000 workers in the cotton industry, yet the returns show that only three-fifths of them worked in factories. In all the census counted 1,176,000 textile workers but, as the table shows, only around half were engaged in factory work.

Coal
Other sectors of the economy saw significant continuity in terms of technology and methods of production. Production and the manufacture of goods increased in the period 1820–51 because of the ability to increase supply using the existing technology and because the demand for goods rose with a growing population. A case in point is the coal industry.

Increase in demand causes technological change
The spread of steam engines, the coming of the railways and the increase in population provided the dynamic of demand. But the technology of coal production remained largely unchanged. The problem of pumping out mines had been solved by the introduction of steam pumping but until the 1840s the most commonly used pump was Newcomen's rather than Watt's. The problems of poor ventilation and hauling coal were yet to be solved. In 1820 some 17.4 million tons of coal were produced in Britain; by 1850 that figure had risen to 49.4 million tons. However, it was the increase in demand which should be seen as revolutionary and not the means by which that demand was met. Innovations such as Humphrey Davy's safety lamp or John Buddle's air fans took some time to spread. By 1851 coal was dug and often hauled by hand. Indeed, while the number of miners increased from 118,000 in 1841 to 219,000 by 1851, productivity per man actually fell. In the mid-nineteenth century the relative abundance of labour meant that capitalists had little encouragement to invest in labour-saving devices.

Iron

The improvements in the iron industry were most obviously connected to the increase in the scale of the existing technology, most noticeably the blast furnace. Improvements such as James Neilson's hot blast **smelting** process had an instant impact in some areas, especially Scotland; in other areas it took time to be introduced. By 1840 only two-fifths of furnaces in Britain had changed to the new method of smelting. The reason for this was that the main benefit of the hot blast process was that it could be used with coal thought to be of a previously unacceptably low level of carbon. Some areas such as south Wales were slow to catch on to the new technology because the costs of smelting were already low. As important in reducing the cost of iron was the fierce competition which drove prices down.

KEY TERM

Smelting Iron ore is heated and most of the impurities are removed.

Various other improvements in the process of making iron were, again, simple adaptations of existing technology. Most refining of iron was achieved by the **puddling** process. By 1830 the introduction of wet puddling in the Black Country increased the yield of wrought iron from pig iron by lining the puddling hearths with calcined puddling furnace slag. As with so many other industries, the impetus for innovation was somewhat overshadowed by the increase in demand, especially from the railways. From the mid-1830s to 1847, British output of pig iron doubled to 2 million tons a year. Yet the dynamic for this growth was not innovation but the increase in demand. An exception to this argument was Naysmith's steam hammer, invented in 1839, which speeded up the process of forging iron.

KEY TERM

Puddling Molten (liquid) iron is stirred to remove all the impurities.

The change in contemporary perceptions

The factory system did change contemporary perceptions. It involved enormous change as with the demise of the hand loom weaver. However, the industrial engineer in the mid-nineteenth century was as much a tool bearer as a machine minder. Taking Britain as a whole, only 19 per cent of the workforce were in mechanised industry in 1841.

WHAT WAS THE EFFECT OF THE FACTORY SYSTEM ON WOMEN AND THE FAMILY?

Contemporary commentators such as the moralist Lord Ashley or the socialist Freidrich Engels pointed to the employment of women in factories as destroying the family. However, such a view was as much one produced to back up political ideas as reflecting the reality of the role of women.

The effects of industrialisation on women

Such a pessimistic view as the one held by Engels contradicts the census returns which show that the proportion of married women within the factory system was not so high. In Preston in 1851 some 51 per cent of married women worked in the mills. Nationally, 247,705 women were registered as cotton workers by this census. However, as cotton was the only major industry with a large number of married women working regularly it should be concluded that in this period the employment of women generally was partial and occupationally and geographically limited. The vast majority of married women worked primarily within the context of their familial role. This view has been backed up by the work of N.J. Smesler who challenged the idea that industrial change destroyed the extended family of the pre-industrial period and replaced it with a nuclear family based on consumption rather than production. Smesler showed, as did the historian M. Anderson, that within the new factories the family continued to perform an economic role. Often the male mule spinner would use assistance from his own kin. In Preston in 1851, 23 per cent of households had living-in kin who were necessary for factory work. While it is likely that industrialisation transformed the nature of the family group, the pessimism of contemporaries that the family unit had been destroyed should be treated with scepticism.

CONCLUSION

There was significant economic change in the period 1820–51. Some industries benefited from technological innovation. However, by 1851 the majority of employment continued in small-scale handicraft industries. While there was growth, there was not the overall leap forward in production.

Population growth provided the demand for the expansion of industry and the prosperity of certain sectors of agriculture. This growth was based in the growing industrial areas and its main cause was the increasing fecundity of the urban working classes. Such population growth was to provide a large pool of cheap labour which reduced the incentives for entrepreneurs to invest in more efficient and labour-saving machinery.

As overall economic expansion was gradual, so a substantial change in the standard of living of the population is not noticeable until the mid-1840s.

A2 ASSESSMENT

SOURCES ASSIGNMENTS

Example 1 in the style of Edexcel – Radicalism and the British State: The Chartist experience 1838–50.

Reading. For help in answering this question you should read Chapter 10 (pages 79–90) and Section 5 (pages 184–191) in this book.

Study Sources A to F and then read the following questions

Source A

It was the discontent with the Whigs and their législation which helps to explain the absence of an alliance with the middle-class radicals in the Anti-Corn Law League. Although repeal of the Corn Laws was in the economic interest of the working classes, there was no support from the Chartists for the Anti-Corn Law League. Chartism received little support from the middle class. Many middle-class members of the Chartist movement such as Thomas Attwood or the Reverend J. R. Stephens eventually left the movement because they could not accept the idea of universal male suffrage. There were attempts by middle-class radicals to form an alliance with Chartists. However they failed because of the fundamental and deep-seated divisions between those who had political power and those who did not.

Adapted from Martin Collier and Philip Pedley, *Britain 1815–1851*, 2001.

Source B

It is vital to appreciate two things [about Chartism]: it was a political movement and a genuinely national one . . . Discussions of the reasons why Chartism 'took off' in the late 1830s so often concentrate on economic and social factors: rising food prices, economic depression and reactions to the Poor Law Amendment Act of 1834 . . . Chartism was nourished by a long-established radical tradition, stretching back to at least the 1790s and the so-called 'artisan radicalism' which took its inspiration from the French Revolution. None of the Chartists' 'Six Points' was new. Most had been widely debated by radical politicians for at least half a century. They were all political. If Chartism was merely a reaction to bad times for working people . . . why were all of the six points political? The Chartist petitions to parliament did not call for a minimum wage, for additional rights for trade unionists or for the abolition of the hated new Poor Law.

Adapted from Eric Evans, *Chartism Revisited* from *History Review*, 1999.

Source C

From small and identifiable origins Chartism widened into a mass of activities . . . It floated [as] a collection of working class movements with different objectives, different philosophies, different grievances and different leaders. The Charter provided nothing new in the way of political thought; and less than was commonly thought in the way of united action. Underneath were still the old complicated phenomena of classes, trades and regions, mass meetings, religious revivalism, the popular press, physical violence and constitutional agitation. The more the Chartists exhibited the aggressive proletarian nature of their movement, the more the middle class doubted their fitness to exercise the parliamentary franchise. Though Chartism was in one sense only a continuation under another name of the old radical reform movement and was to last in some shape or other into the 1850s, what gave it contemporary importance was the great industrial depression from 1837 to 1843 . . . Hungry bellies filled the ranks of the Chartists; the return of economic prosperity after 1843 thinned them.

Adapted from Norman Gash, *Aristocracy and People*, 1979.

Source D

The few have governed in the interests of the few, while the interests of the many have been neglected or trampled upon. It was the fond expectation of friends of the people that a remedy for their grievances would be found in the Reform Act of 1832. They have been bitterly and basely deceived. The Reform Act has effected a transfer of power from one domineering faction to another and left the people as helpless as before.

We come before your Honourable House to tell you, with all humility, that this state of things cannot long continue without seriously endangering the stability of the throne and the peace of the kingdom. Universal suffrage will, and it alone can, bring true and lasting peace to the nation; we firmly believe that it will also bring prosperity.

Adapted from the Chartist Petition, 1839.

Source E

I shall this night be engaged in a glorious struggle for freedom, and should it please God to spare my life, I shall see you see; but if not grieve not for me, I shall have fallen in a noble cause.

Adapted from a letter by George Shell to his parents, written in 1839.
Shell was a Chartist killed in the Newport Rising.

Questions

1 Study Sources A, C and E. Please refer to all three sources in your answer. Using your own knowledge and the evidence of these three sources explain what you consider were the main reasons why Chartism failed. (15)

How to answer this question. Your answer will be marked on the following criteria:

- The recall and clear communication of historical knowledge.
- The quality of explanation and the judgements that you make in response to the question.
- The ability to draw conclusions from the sources and use them effectively.

Plan. After studying the question you should read through the sources and identify any reasons why Chartism failed which are suggested in each. This will help you to outline your main points of argument in your plan.

Style. Below is an example of the style of writing you might choose to use in answering this type of question. You should note that the extract attempts to follow the advice given above in the 'How to answer this question' section.

If one argues that Chartism was a reflection of the Whigs' rule in Britain in the 1830s then real reform or perceived change to the system undermined the Chartist movement. The 'class legislation' of the 1830s, e.g. the new Poor Law was not repeated in the 1840s. Instead Peel in particular introduced legislation which was less oppressive, the Mines Act of 1842 was followed by the Repeal of the Corn Laws in 1846, a Ten-Hours Act in 1847 and the abolition of the hated Poor Law Commission in 1847. Chartism began to fail as a coherent critique of the political system when the urgency for political change became less apparent in the eyes of its supporters. The movement also began to fail when economic conditions improved, as is suggested by Source C: 'Hungry bellies filled the ranks of the Chartists; the return of economic prosperity after 1843 thinned them'.

2 How far do you agree with the author of Source B that Chartism was 'a political movement and a genuinely national one'? Use the evidence of all five sources and your own knowledge to answer the question. (15)

How to answer this question. This question focuses on the idea of the making and supporting of a historical interpretation. Your task is to make and support a judgement about the validity of this interpretation. To answer this question successfully you must try to do the following:

- Show that you can draw on your understanding of a range of historical interpretations. This does not mean that you simply write out what different historians have said. Historiographical 'own knowledge' is not in itself a requirement for the highest level. However, if you integrate an awareness of the debate into your argument then that information will be rewarded as will be all other 'own knowledge'.
- You need to show that you can link your own knowledge and the information from all of the sources.
- You need to answer this question directly. The question is 'how far' and the answer, therefore, is 'to a certain extent but . . .'.

Plan. Before you start writing you need to draw up a plan with your main points of argument. It is important that these points directly answer the question.

- The Charter and its central importance in the movement do, indeed, point to the Charter being primarily political in nature.
- Although there were different strands of Chartism, it is also accurate to describe the movement as a national one because of the common cause, which was the success of the Charter.
- However, one should qualify the statement. While primarily political, Chartism arose against a backdrop of economic depression. The movement also had important divisions which reflected regional variations.

Style. Below is an example of the style of writing you might adopt. The answer attempts to argue in response to the question, develop an interpretation, select from the source and recall knowledge.

It is clear that the Chartist movement had at its heart a critique of the political nation. The main points of the Charter all relate to an improvement of the political system. Thus it was described by Evans in Source B who argues strongly that Chartism should be seen as primarily political in nature for the movement, as Evans writes 'was nourished by a long-established radical tradition'. This again can be seen in the language of the Charter which contradicts the belief promoted by J.R. Stephens that Chartism was a 'knife and fork' matter. The 1839 Charter identifies the central issue of Chartism as being the monopoly of political power; 'the few have governed in the interests of the few while the interests of the many have been neglected or trampled upon'.

Essay questions

Types of essay questions asked in the A2 specifications. The great majority of history questions fall into two categories:

- The first category of questions is those which essentially require a reason-based approach. By this it is meant that you are to examine the reasons for a particular phenomenon. In these answers it is most useful to include some form of comparison of points and you should most definitely prioritise both positively and negatively.

    Examples of these types of questions are those which ask:

    Why?
    What are the reasons?
    Explain . . .

- The second category of questions are those which demand the answer 'up to a point . . . but'.

    Examples of these types of questions are those which ask:

    Consider the view . . .
    To what extent?

Plan. You should be able to plan your questions by recognising which of the two categories the question you are asked comes from. If the question is from the first category, you plan your answer by arguing a prioritisation of the reasons. If the question is from the second category, your line of argument should take the line of 'up to a point . . . but'.

Exception. The only exceptions are questions which ask why, *and* to what extent . . . ?

To answer these questions you must mix the two, plan for two answers and split your answer accordingly. In a sense this question demands two responses in one essay.

How to write an essay. To be awarded top marks in essays of the type given below, you will be expected to do the following:

- Analyse throughout the essay. This can be done by making sure that you plan a line of argument before you start writing. At the start of each paragraph you must make the next point of your argument, explain it and then use evidence to back up your point (see next point). There is a clear difference between narrative (telling the story) and analysis (putting forward a reasoned argument in response to a question).

A tip for how to ensure that you are analysing. You need to start each paragraph with words which will lead onto analysis. These might include:

The most important reason . . .
Another key point is that . . .
One should argue that . . .
Essentially . . .

If you use the following words at the start of a paragraph you are more likely to fall into a narrative style of writing:

In (followed by a date) . . .
This was followed by . . .

- Back up your argument by using well selected evidence. The evidence you select must be accurate and relevant to the point you are trying to make.
- Make a clear and consistent attempt to reach a judgement. In your essay you must argue throughout. You must reflect on the evidence you have given and make points which answer the question directly.
- Show evidence of independent thought. You do not have to be original. Independent thought means that you have reflected on what you have read in this and other books and that you can explain the ideas that you have picked up in your own words.
- Language skills. It is essential that you write in paragraphs, and that you are grammatically accurate. There are two tips to ensure this takes place:

Always read your work through after you have finished and correct any errors.
Get into the habit of structuring your essays in such a way that a new point of your argument means a new paragraph.

Questions in the style of Edexcel (Unit 4 – Tory men and Tory measures)

1 Why did Castlereagh join the Congress System so wholeheartedly and to what extent were Britain's interests well served by the Congress System in the period 1815–22? (20)

How to answer this question. This is a two-part question and you should attempt to draw up a plan which deals effectively with both halves. You might include a discussion of most of the following points:

- What were Britain's interests after 1815 and how far might they have altered?
- Castlereagh's personal objectives in foreign policy.
- The importance of the Congress System for Britain.
- Whether Britain had common interest with the autocratic powers.
- The significance of trade in formulating British foreign policy.

> **3** To what extent did the work of Peel and Huskisson in the period 1822–27 suggest that Lord Liverpool's administration could be described as being 'liberal'. (20)

How to answer this question. This is a question which demands an 'up to a point . . . but' style of answer, i.e. that Lord Liverpool's government was 'liberal' 'up to a point, but'.

Style. Here is an extract from an answer to this question. Note that the candidate has attempted to be direct in answering the question.

However, while it is wrong to assume that 'Liberal Toryism' represented any major ideological shift or inspired series of radical reforms it should not be dismissed out of hand. 'Liberal Toryism' does reflect a more tolerant and imaginative and well-informed approach to social and economic problems and in this sense can be described as 'liberal'. In some areas 'Liberal Tories' introduced reforms of great significance. The establishment of a Metropolitan Police Force in 1829 reflected a new maturity and understanding of the causes of social unrest. By setting up a police force the government recognised that social problems could not be addressed with a combination of spies, informers and local yeomanry. Equally important were the repeal of the Test and Corporations Act of 1828 and the granting of Catholic emancipation in 1829. By removing civil and political disabilities the Tories appeased Catholic unrest in Ireland and helped remove sectarian bitterness from English politics.

BIBLIOGRAPHY

The books listed below are recommended for use for both AS and A2.

P. Adelman, *Peel and the Conservative Party, 1830-1850*, Longman (1989)

A. Briggs, *The Age of Improvement, 1793-1867*, Longman (second edition 2000)

A.M. Brock, *The Great Reform Act*, Hutchinson (1973)

H. Browne, *Chartism*, Hodder & Stoughton (1999)

M.E. Chamberlain, *British Foreign Policy in the Age of Palmerston*, Longman (1980)

E. Evans, *Sir Robert Peel: Statesmanship, Power and Party*, Routledge (1994)

E. Evans, *The Forging of the Modern State – Early Industrial Britain, 1783-1867*, Longman (1983)

N. Gash, *Aristocracy and People – Britain 1815-1865*, Edward Arnold (1979)

N. Gash, *Peel*, Longman (1976)

T.R. Gourvish, *Railways and the British Economy: 1830-1914*, Macmillan (1980)

S. Lee, *Aspects of British Political History, 1815-1914*, Routledge (1994)

T. May, *An Economic and Social History of Britain, 1760-1970*, Longman (1987)

J. Plowright, *Regency England: The Age of Lord Liverpool*, Routledge (1996)

R. Rees, *Poverty and Public Health: 1815-1914*, Heinemann (2001)

M. Scott-Baumann (ed.), *Years of Expansion: 1815-1914*, Hodder & Stoughton (1995)

D. Thompson, *The Chartists*, Temple Smith (1984)

E.P. Thompson, *The Making of the English Working Class*, Pelican (1968)

N. Tonge, *Industrialisation and Society 1700-1914*, Nelson (1993)

E. Royle, *Chartism*, Longman Seminar Series (1986)

J.T. Ward, *Popular Movements c. 1830-1850*, Macmillan (1970)

D. Watts, *Tories, Conservatives and Unionists*, Hodder & Stoughton (1994)

INDEX